THE DARKENING GREEN

Our authorised representative in the EU for product safety is
Easy Access System Europe, Mustamäe tee 50, 10621 Tallinn, Estonia
gpsr.requests@easproject.com

The Darkening Green

ELIZABETH CLARKE

ff
faber and faber

This edition first published in 2012
by Faber and Faber Ltd
Bloomsbury House, 74–77 Great Russell Street
London WC1B 3DA

Printed by Books on Demand GmbH, Norderstedt

All rights reserved
© Elizabeth Clarke, 1964

The decorations in this book
were engraved on wood
by Richard Shirley Smith

The right of Elizabeth Clarke to be identified as author of this work
has been asserted in accordance with Section 77 of the
Copyright, Designs and Patents Act 1988

This book is sold subject to the condition that it shall not, by way of
trade or otherwise, be lent, resold, hired out or otherwise circulated
without the publisher's prior consent in any form of binding or cover other than
that in which it is published and without a similar condition including this
condition being imposed on the subsequent purchaser

A CIP record for this book is available from the British Library

ISBN 978–0–571–29522–7

ACKNOWLEDGEMENTS

I particularly want to thank Dr Ivy Williams for her kindness in allowing me to quote from her Braille Course and her letters. I would also like to thank all the other people who have helped this book forward. Each will know who is meant.

My grateful acknowledgement is due to the following for kind permission to include these extracts:

The Literary Trustees for Walter de la Mare and The Society of Authors as their representative for 'Fare Well', from COLLECTED POEMS, by Walter de la Mare, the last verse.

Mrs Alida Monro for 'Midnight Lamentation', by Harold Monro, the first three and last two verses.

The Trustees of the Hardy Estate and Macmillan & Company Ltd. for 'The Oxen', from THE COLLECTED POEMS OF THOMAS HARDY, the last two verses.

E. C.

PREFACE TO SECOND IMPRESSION

This book is the experience of two people personified in an imaginary third, for it was written when my husband's sight partially failed, and 'Lucy Shebbear' participates in his approach to vision by senses independent of sight, and in my grounding in farm and country life. So, while the tale evolved in imagination, the experience is fact.

E. C.

NOTE

The notebook from which this scene is drawn ended ten years ago, before myxomatosis destroyed the rabbits, and before main electricity reached the remote farms of Devon. I have left unchanged certain ways of speech which have no sanction from the dictionary, and depend on the countryman's authority; and I have filled in some details of the figures who moved with me about my diminishing landscape, so that the reader may better enjoy their company. But if he should look for them he will not find their exact originals. He might catch glimpses of them in the farmhouses, outbuildings, cottages and inns of the country that borders Dartmoor, and coming upon some field or yard or lane I hope he may fancy he has been there before.

L. S.
July 1962

Look thy last on all things lovely,
Every hour. Let no night
Seal thy sense in deathly slumber
　Till to delight
Thou have paid thy utmost blessing;
Since that all things thou wouldst praise
Beauty took from those who loved them
　In other days.

From 'Fare Well', by Walter de la Mare

 I

Late in the afternoon my father met me at the station. It was clear from his attitude—as though he had taken root—that he had been there for at least ten minutes rather than be late, and it gave me something to say, for from the platform he would have been looking over acres of fields and in his mind's eye he was sure to have been farming other men's land. I made some joke about it, and he rose to the occasion with his cautious smile, saying that some farmers could not raise anything except their hats. He gave me a searching look before I climbed into the old car, but instead of saying any more he walked round it, giving all the tyres a kick with the side of his boot to make sure that none of them was soft, arming himself, as he had by his over-punctual arrival at the station, against mishap. Before starting the engine he tried the traffic signals, then we drove slowly out of the yard.

Except for the only thing he would not ask we had no need for enquiry. Since the morning he had added to the clothes he had been wearing when I left—an old and weathered tweed jacket over a shirt with a stud in the front of the collarband, cord trousers and leather boots—the sunburnt panama hat which he takes out every year for haymaking, and so I knew that he had spent the day, while I had been away, cutting the first field. Saving the hay, the local name for hay harvest, might have been coined by my father with his sense of urgency and fear of misfortune.

When we stopped before turning into the lane leading to the farm he looked at me closely again. 'So they didn't give you spectacles?' he said.

'No,' I answered; and added unnecessarily, 'they didn't give me spectacles.'

Again, before he turned the car under the arch that leads into the yard, he said: 'So they didn't think you needed anything?'

'No,' I said. 'Nothing.'

In the middle of every morning a train dawdles along the valley at the bottom of the farm, skirting the Moor; the train which I caught today. As it passes, workers, who do not bother to look up, consider the time—two hours to dinner. Except during holiday time it carries very few strangers. Its passengers are mostly women who embark on windswept stations where ferns grow between granite blocks on the sides of the platforms, who read the actions of men working in the fields, instead of newspapers, and could say what crop every field along the line has carried for the last three or four years, though if questioned by their menfolk they would return a scornful answer; it is not their habit to give away their observation of outdoor work. With gifts of exquisitely trussed fowls, and carefully chosen eggs, and butter made to defy criticism, they are out on visits to friends and relations; and I was conspicuous with only my handbag.

'Where be going, Lucy?' my neighbour asked. But while I answered vaguely we passed our farm, and her attention was diverted.

Three weeks ago I stood in the highest of our fields looking, without anxiety, at the grass which today was cut for hay. It was little more than ankle-deep then, enclosed by hedges cascading in mayflowers, and trees in small leaf still allowing glimpses of distant pastures through their branches. Then it was coloured with the burnished petals of buttercups and grassheads almost brown, sorrel with flowers the colour of coral beads, cinnamon-coloured plantain heads, cuckoo flowers of faded lilac, the grey down of dandelion clocks; and among the leaves of all the flowers and grass, and silverweed like crumpled yellow roses with feathered, frosted leaves, a daisy or two. The grassheads darkened the surface like varnish, and as the wind blew over them they rippled away like the tide lapping up a shallow beach.

A fly flew into my right eye, and while I tried to remove it I found that the trees had developed a semicircular bend in their trunks. When the drowned fly was disposed of I looked with both eyes and all was well, but when I looked again with only the left eye the distortion repeated itself.

During a week of disbelief, of testing, of forgetfulness, of remembering, and the nights' oblivion, I found that all vertical lines developed the same bend when seen only with the left eye, and that in a book I saw a shadow about the size of one of the old silver threepenny pieces, the top edge just covering the word immediately below the one I was looking at. But time, who has always been my master, pursuing me in the small round of the household within the wide circle of the farming seasons, released me briefly, allowing me to persuade myself that there was no hurry. Yet, one day during the weeks while spring matured to summer, I went to our doctor who gave me a letter to deliver at the appointment I kept today.

'You've a nice lot of geese this year,' my neighbour said, continuing the speculative farming I had interrupted. 'You set your eggs under hens, I suppose. I never leave my broodies loose,' she mused. 'I shut 'em in their boxes. One may come off, else, and go back on another nest, then the other don't know what to do. They don't like changing nesses.'

She sat squarely in her good felt hat and Harris tweed suit, her comfortable talk flowing on while the summer fields streamed slowly past the windows. We discussed the best age for geese, and neither of us knew. Some people say they remain good for twenty years. We considered the age of ganders and the best colour, and agreed in preferring pure white. Her gander is young, with a grey feather or two in white plumage, and this year all the geese have laid clear eggs. 'He do go for people, all right. Er'll go for a car,' she said with reluctant admiration. 'He does all the things a gander ought to do, 'cep' one.'

At every station there were partings and meetings and messages called to friends. Someone asked a stationmaster to telephone to a farmer down the line that one of his sheep was on its back. At last we all parted on Exeter station until we should meet again on the train that would dawdle us home in time to pick up the eggs.

My father turned the car under the arch and roared the engine to a standstill in the implement shed. If I should never see it again I should remember every detail of the yard: the long house facing the arch, and the buildings on each side joining them to enclose half an acre of red earth in an unembattled fortress. And in the mind's eye the cushions of moss on the slate roofs of the buildings would start out of the picture with the magic proportions of childhood: pincushion shapes of hearts and fans and moons the colour of green plush, dry now, but brilliant in the dove-light of damp, sunless spring days, drenched with the moisture that holds back tilling and dulls ploughland worn smooth by frost and rain. And an elastic population of cats would emerge suddenly from tunnels in the stacked hay in the tallets under the roofs, and pour itself, like a migration of eels, down the walls of calf pens and foodstores, pigsties, the shippon and the implement shed, as it has since I can remember, every morning and evening, when the ring of a bucket on the floor of the dairy announces the first preparations for milking.

Hens pick about in the yard, taking one step forward to scratch earth rutted with the crescent footmarks of cattle, and a step backward to search with oblique glances in dust red as the buildings that surround them, made of the same red earth mixed with straw and cowhair, standing on a base of stone. Even the house, which has been whitewashed, obstinately shows the red beneath, making it patchily rose-coloured under the last thatch left on the farm, dark as fur. Doors of oak strips the width of trees defend the buildings, and a low iron railing protects the house from the ponderous curiosity of the cows whose languid progress into the yard never carries them straight to the shippon, but drives them instead, meditatively swinging their tails and moving heavy heads, to look round with sudden alertness for something to investigate, steal, or knock over, while they wait for the end of the slow procession followed by my father or his aged helper, Dick Meldon.

There was no one in the yard when we put the car away, and I hurried into the house, leaving my father to linger over jobs he had really finished. The stone steps up to the door had been scrubbed, and the cobbled floor of the passage shone like a grey, pebbled shore. I guessed that Dick had sluiced and broomed them, as a sympathetic gesture—though it is a job usually done only on Saturdays—before leaving for the night; but the kitchen was as reserved as a deserted church, blank as a face asleep.

If my father had had a son, his bride would probably have succeeded to the kitchen before now, while we moved into 'the gentleman's side', the front of the house. Then there would almost certainly have been changes in the kitchen. But as it is, a black three-gallon kettle still hangs on a crook in the wide fireplace which a young farmer's wife would have filled with a modern grate; the oak dresser with its burden of china, the old ladder-back chairs, and the huge kitchen table with a bench along one side, have not been replaced by a Suite; and my mother's ladylike water-colours, painted before her marriage and brought here as proof of a leisurely education, still decorate the walls alternately with the more solid evidence of prize-winning certificates for cake-making. Only the muslin-shrouded hams and shoulders and backs of bacon hanging from the ceiling beams are replaced from time to time by the successors of scores, probably hundreds, of cuts of bacon that have gone. . . .

But I had no time to coax the room back to familiarity, and brusquely opened a drawer of the dresser to take out the first tablecloth that came under my hand, an old-fashioned damask cloth which I shook out and spread on the table under the window commanding the yard, where the light pounced on the pattern in its threads.

Why should pillars of roses, woven into a square of linen, suddenly remind me that my father pursues his quiet life armed to the teeth? This cloth was one of my mother's, brought from the Moor farm of her childhood to the farm which my father expected to inherit. I was spoon-fed in a high chair above those roses while they were stained red by the earthy forearms of my irascible old grandfather, my father, and his younger brother; and I cannot have been far away in the moment of aghast surprise when the old man's will was read, leaving his farm to the younger son.

I have never known the reason for my father's disinheritance, but unbreachable quarrels are not more unusual between farmers and their eldest sons than between the gentry and theirs; for where the family's livelihood depends on physical labour, the son, gaining strength as his father's declines, yields less willingly, in the almost inevitable clashes between youth and age, to the force of experience and adherence to old methods. When I was a year old these roses were spread on the table of a farm worker's cottage on another farm. I was three when another will, made with the almost primitive secrecy of the first, put my father in possession of this farm. It had belonged to his aunt, and she may have framed her will to right a wrong, or to score off her fiery elder brother, or because of the mere chance that their initials were the same: Judith Beer, John Belstone.

No family sociability passes between the two farms. The hazard that made my father a farmer again did not relax the lines of caution engraved on his face, nor intensify the quiet voice and careful gestures that give the appearance of stealth, though during the forty-five years that have worn this cloth brittle and thin he has farmed his land with dogged efficiency for forty-one, smiled at for his astringent jokes, and followed, secretly, in his yearly plan of tillage, for every man's fields are an open book to his neighbours. Fifteen years ago my mother reluctantly deserted her kitchen for two days, before she died of pneumonia, and my father strengthened his defences for what he believed was the last time.

When I raised my eyes from the table, the mother cat, Matriarch of the tribe, was sitting on the dresser, erect and formal, her tabby lines falling into a pattern of bracelets and necklaces. Her eyes, cynical and appraising, had been bent on the back of my head, and as I met her glance it said, as ever, 'We understand one another', though I have never known whether she draws comfort or derisive amusement from the thought; for, as I face her, the narrow eyes widen, and her expression becomes falsely open and frank. But I wondered, then, whether the intuition that leads her ahead on errands I have scarcely had time to plan had told her what had happened.

When my father came in to tea I meant to break my news to him after we had finished, and I asked him how he had managed in my absence, with Nancy, our occasional helper, cooking his dinner. She had done her best, he said, but with me away she could not—he imitated her hit-or-miss vocabulary—consecrate on it.

He held off his anxiety, for as long as he could, with his armoury of austere little jokes, but he was outmatched. 'It seemed a long time, Lucy,' he said.

Then the brass handles on the drawers of the dark dresser shot out, winking, towards me, the hams and shoulders of bacon seemed to close round my head, the tablecloth to rise up and stifle me, and I was not sitting at the table opposite him any longer, but standing behind his chair, holding the curtain aside as though it were urgent that I should see out into the yard. But instead of the yard I saw a momentary picture of our window as people passing in the lane see it in autumn and winter: of my father and me framed above a lake of darkness, eating our tea by lamplight. I said: 'In three months I shall be almost blind.'

Within the room the quiet atmosphere rippled as ring succeeds ring when a stone is dropped into still water, until my father broke the heavy silence, jerking back his chair with a violent thrust of ironshod heels, saying, 'Come out in the fields.'

I thought, as we left our half-eaten meal, that it was better for my father that this blow should have fallen on his daughter than on his wife, for only one of his own blood would be likely to share his need for the open air in time of crisis. A farmer's wife's house is her refuge, and I remembered my mother's indignation when a town visitor who had come to tea had told her excitedly, 'I would love this wild life!'

'Wild life!' my mother repeated scornfully, her glance round her apple-pie kitchen gathering her household treasures about her. 'I don't see nothing wild about it!' But her very indignation betrayed her. She belonged to a generation of farmers' wives who devoted their lives to keeping the fields and the yard in their proper place. The shining cobbles in the passage which Father and Dick would not have thought of passing without kicking their boots off, the gleaming linoleum and the matting covering the cobbled kitchen floor, the satin polish on the furniture, the blazing winter fire and stintless baking, even my father's defiantly shabby armchair, diffused a feeling of well-being that amounted to luxury in my mother's care. And though she and her neighbours interested themselves in poultry and calves and other outside things, indoors, aproned and often hatted, they presented a formal demeanour that shut out muck and rough weather almost as effectively as their ceaseless battle against them.

In the yard gnats danced in the evening sunshine, spinning up and down, weaving and turning, yet never leaving the vertical pattern of their dance, sheltered from the light airs that rippled over the pasture and in the trees and strayed to carry from distant fields voices that died as the wind dropped. In that more open atmosphere I told my father what the specialist had said about my eyes—that the small blood vessels at the back of the eye, no thicker than a hair, had broken and were still bleeding, and that when the bleeding stopped they would heal leaving scars which I should not be able to see through; that I should see nothing in a straight line because the scars would be in the line of vision; that I should be able neither to read nor to see clearly then.

My father had not spoken since we left the house, and I

hoped he would not say anything now. But he lifted his intent gaze from the field we had reached, which he had cut during the day.

'Ah well,' he said, with an effort at cheerfulness, 'us should be thankful 'tis only one eye.'

'I'm afraid it's not,' I said. 'The same thing has begun in the other.'

We had come, without premeditation, to the highest point of the farm and looked over the cut hay and the lilac glow of a beanfield, over fields of rippling grass and swaying flowers, green fields of corn and great shoulders of red land, to the Moor, rising in blue mountains. The scent of beanflowers drifted in our faces and died again.

'Would you like us to sell the farm and settle in a little place?' my father asked with forced enthusiasm.

'We'd suffocate,' I said. 'Besides, we've had that out before. Here on a winter day. When Richard died.'

We came to this place ten years ago after hearing that my husband's bomber had crashed over Germany, and while we stared over an expressionless landscape of raw ploughed fields and sallow winter pastures towards the Moor, lost in the colourless sky, my father had made the same suggestion, and I had answered that we would hang on as long as we had strength. He had replied with the rare smile that gratefully undid the caustic lines of his mouth, though caution forced him, talking broad, as he always has when moved, to say: 'Us've no future, Lucy.'

'We have the farm,' I had said.

The hay lay in long swaths now, gently curving to the contour of the land, with flowers fading among the grasses—ragged robin and sorrel, buttercups and ryegrass, foxtail and sweet vernal grass, cocksfoot, fescue and meadowgrass, curing, tarnishing already to the colour of neglected silver.

'When we talked about this before, you said we'd still have the farm,' my father said. 'But if you can't see you won't have it, will ee, the way you meant?'

Meadow Brown butterflies that haunt a hayfield, following one another over its shining surface, weaving in and out among the flowering grassheads to flirt and settle and make love, dipped and mourned over the lying swaths. On the headlands flowers and lush grasses moved in the light air with a hushing sound, and the wind spoke in the heavy elms on the banks. But it had no voice in the fallen hay as it had in the field whose responsive face once moved, moved, like water under its touch.

'I believe I can keep it in my mind as long as I live,' I said.

Before moonlight. While I write, to enrich my memory, in a book that I shall not read, the sun has sunk in the valley, and a full moon the colour of lamplight stands in the south. But the only light on earth falls from the sky, which is clear and blue, the moon still holding her radiance within herself.

Hedges and trees are dark, the fields are grey with dew, and there is no difference now in colour between the living green of young corn, the pale, cropped pastures, and the browning hayfields that ripple all day before the wind. The few bare fields of red land are the same veiled grey as the beanfield that moves and rustles all day breathing drifts of sweet air, humming with bees in the black-spotted blossoms. White flowers, foaming along the hedge bottoms, meet the pale gaze of drooping elder, where foxglove and campion are hidden in darkness beside the dusty heads of bending nettles and the brilliant carpet, at the fields' verges, of the small flowers that follow the plough: forget-me-not, hop trefoil and bedstraw, pimpernel and cranesbill, creeping industriously to preserve themselves from suffocation by stronger weeds, urgently covering the rutted earth with a clash of blue and yellow, lavender, scarlet, and cyclamen.

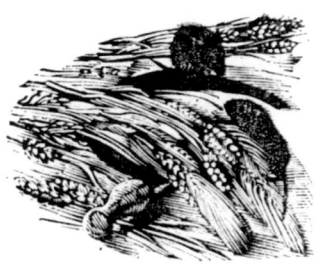

2

'The dog jumped out of the hedge, ravin' and making a calamity.' Nancy was at the sink in the back kitchen, bathing her bruised calf where her neighbour's dog had snapped at her as she passed on her bicycle. She had come to ask what the doctor had said to me yesterday, and wept when I told her. She suggested that perhaps my eyes might grow better, but added, before I could reply, 'No, that's what I used to think about my funny foot. It was just another of my daft ideals, like I used to think the gentry never quarrelled.'

For years the incongruous diversity of Nancy's vocabulary has been a joy to Father and me; but today a new awareness discovered, for the first time, how brightly its decorations contrast with any allusion to the lameness which contributes a sombre thread to the otherwise cheerful, haphazard pattern of her existence. The hardly noticeable drag in her tread, her skipping step when she is in a hurry, would be dismissed as personal idiosyncrasy if her father, who was by nature the kind of individualist who tends to be always up against his equals, had not been lamed by a severe fall before she was born, when he was thrown by a bolting horse off a loaded cart, while helping a neighbour to save his hay. After the accident his natural independence expanded into eccentricity, and his bouts of odd behaviour gained him the reputation of being mad. Any reference to her lameness, by Nancy's neighbours, contains hints of an inheritance of madness, and if she talks about her disability or her father's trouble it is in guarded understatement as 'my funny foot' or 'Dad's awkward turns', as though to conceal from a listening Fate any reminder of her vulnerability.

'Who does this dog belong to?' I asked.

'The Wrangways,' she said. 'It's Gloucester Wrangways's dog.'

'Have you told him?'

She raised her round, comely face, and her dark eyes met mine for agreement. 'No,' she said. 'They'd hit it. Besides,' she added conclusively, 'I'm not speaking to they no more.'

'Why not?'

She dabbed her bruised leg roughly. 'They say I shouldn't have married Jim. They say I might go funny.'

I changed the subject, suggesting that I had always thought Gloucester an odd name, knowing that if I argued she would shut out the invasion of common sense from her stronghold of ancient beliefs. We have a distant blood relationship—a connection such as elders delight in clarifying, with contradictions and counter-suggestions, at weddings and funerals. But our mutual understanding has a more obvious foundation: we were bred on the same soil, rich in the folklore and superstition which repay stubborn observance with the promise of security, and visit stealthy punishments on disobedience.

'Is Gloucester his real name?'

'Oh, no,' she said. 'His real name's George.'

'Why's he called Gloucester, then?'

'*I* don't know,' she said comfortably, 'I suppose he's been there.'

In the row of five cottages, half a mile down the lane, where Nancy and her husband live next-door to her mother, curiosity over little things is as busy as a mouse in a storecupboard, but over facts established by long habit the neighbours are as acquiescent as a family. Everyone's day-to-day business is everyone's property. All have a garden at the back, closely cultivated with vegetables under the critical eyes of three other households—Nancy's husband works her mother's garden with his own; each has a washing line scrutinized and remarked on every Monday. Rows break out and neighbours do not speak, angry remarks are heard through cob walls and on doorsteps under windows, then they settle down, and the women gossip again comfortably while they fetch water from the well on the other side of the lane, or 'stream the washing', pumping gallons of clear water, with the long arm of the old sleeve pump, over the clothes they have washed in their kitchens and bring out to put in the stone trough under the spout: Mrs Wrangways, Gloucester's mother, middle-aged and bossy; Nancy's mother, enjoying a soft life after a hard one now that her family has grown up, airily wondering why she didn't leave her washing for Nancy, knowing that she does it better herself; old Mrs Willsworthy, her face rutted like the bark of an oak, refusing help and toddling in again to grumble about the younger women to her husband, whom she calls Father, though they have no family.

One Saturday afternoon in autumn the men lag the pump with straw and sacking: young Gloucester Wrangways, and Nancy's husband, Jim, bending to the work while the old men stand by and smoke and advise and reminisce: Gloucester's father, Archie Wrangways, a weasel of a man in earth-coloured clothes, who, in retirement, does odd jobs on any of the nearby farms that need him; Dick Meldon, our old farm worker, stiff jointed, stooping like a heron, his great frame reduced by age to its bony architecture; old Bill Willsworthy, who was a waggoner on our farm in my great-aunt's time, frail and asthmatic, talking about his horses. When there is a hard frost during the winter the first one out in the morning will unfreeze the pump. Even when they are under their own roofs they are not really independent of one another, for all share the danger of fire from the carelessness of one, since all live under the same thatch.

As all have had very much the same experience of life they measure one another's doings with a practised eye. Each one has an opinion to express about how the others should spend their money, manage their family, or whether Nancy ought to have married Jim; but a nickname, coined perhaps twenty years ago and worn commonplace in circulation, is accepted as uncritically as a personal habit, which is above question. Mrs Wrangways never goes to the village on Tuesdays, Nancy says. Why? She just doesn't.

While Nancy and I sat over our morning cup of tea in the big kitchen the mother cat brought in a mouse, and her two newest kittens played with it, learning the pretty gestures of murder: the soft advance and retreat of a curled paw, the toss and dip and serpentine movements of a cat protracting a winning game.

'When were those kittens born?' Nancy asked.

Last month, I told her.

'May cats bring in snakes,' she said.

Wash in May, wash one of the family away; the seventh child of a seventh child can bless away ringworm and warts; if you are frightened by an animal before you have a baby, the child will have some peculiarity of the creature; a sheep's heart, hanging in the chimney, will keep you from being witched if you stick a pin into it every time a gypsy comes to the door. Superficially, Nancy laughs at the articles of her faith, handed down with examples by her mother; but in her heart she honours them. Even my father will defend them, remembering a bunch of heifers stricken with ringworm, which recovered when the local practitioner blessed them—all except one, which Father had put in a distant byre while the charm was said; and if anyone questions the old beliefs he will tell them about a flock of lambing ewes, disturbed by a dog, whose lambs were born with dog's ears.

'Nancy,' I said, 'have you thought of talking to the doctor about your father's trouble?'

'No,' she said decidedly.

'Don't you think it would be a good idea?'

''Twouldn' be no good,' she replied. 'You don't understand. You'm educated.'

We had come to a dead-end. In childhood, because I was the same age as her daughter Pamela, I was invited by the doctor's wife to share lessons with her matchless governess in the disused vicarage they had recently bought on the other side of the lane. It was an unusual step then, to ask a village child into the house on those terms, questioned, probably, by the gentry, and certainly by my mother's friends; and according to the needs of the moment, during any argument with my own people, my education is referred to, sooner or later, either as an unfair advantage or, in local matters, as a gross handicap.

Nancy, having gained a point, generously decided to explain. 'It's like this, the doctor can't stop things happening, can he? Before my brother Dan was born a bat dropped off the roof in the linhay on to my mother's hand. Well, Mum had a bad leg, and she bent down to rub it, and Danny's got a mole on his leg shaped just like a bat. The doctor couldn't have stopped that, could he?'

'No,' I said, and recognized a red herring too late. 'But, Nancy, your father's trouble had nothing to do with things like that, it was the result of an accident. Why should it be passed on?'

'Other people think it will,' said Nancy doggedly.

While the mother cat washed herself with pretended absorption the kittens were performing an exuberant burlesque of her exquisite mime with the dead mouse, which she affected to ignore; and I knew that I should have to borrow the timeless patience of animals to lure Nancy from her fastness of ancient convictions: the moments of intense perseverance, and long intervals of assumed indifference, of a cat persuading her kittens to make the steep journey down the steps from their first home in the tallet, or of parent birds teaching their young to fend for themselves. I asked her to take care of the dinner I had prepared, while I went to see my mother's old friend, Cicely Rackenford.

'That's a good ideal,' she said cheerfully, straying a little, as usual, in her choice of a word.

In the yard the hum of tractors filled the sunny air, and a lighter sound, the clacking of mowers, was raised like the song of grasshoppers. Everyone was cutting hay. Hidden among trees at the end of a spotless drive opposite the archway, a dog barked in Judge Mowbray's house, joined by the clangour of hounds. Between the drive and the church, ox-eye daisies whitened the graveyard with a gently moving pall, levelling mounds, crowding against lichened stones, stooping over the wall to the lane. Beyond the church the gate of the Old Vicarage stood open, rotting on its hinges, exposing the moss-covered drive, once immaculate, and the overgrown shrubs leaning over it. A boy's voice shouted from the direction of the house: 'Pete, Si,' and was answered by a shapeless sound: Pamela's boys. Pamela inherited the house at the end of the war, when her husband came out of the army, and with fields rented from Judge Mowbray they turned the place into their idea of a farm.

In almost every life a time must come when stored experience is broached and lived on, like bees' treasure of honey during winter, to tide over some crisis of illness or sorrow or loss. The banks in the lane leaned downwards: flowers and tall grasses and nettles with flowered throats bending towards the road which grows daily narrower. Elder stooped from hedges over banks that matched its creamy flowers with hogweed, earthnut and wild carrot. But as I walked on, towards the Rackenfords' farm, I saw with a flash of retrospect the hedge in the silver days of winter, grey with the polished stems of spiked thorn and rutted oak and smooth and shining ash. I saw banks the colour of old hay, with primroses pressed beneath bent grasses, single faces like pale stars among deeply quilted leaves, the hedge in bud, hardly concealing the round-eyed stares of sitting birds. I saw the lane under a full winter moon, traced with the branched shadows of bare trees across ruts filled with bright water.

Summer does not come early here; we have not the climate of the lush valleys of south Devon; the wind that blows off the Moor holds back the buds. Buzzards slide and circle above bare woods when the southern valleys are in full leaf; and when sheltered country is green, curlews cry their rippling song here above fields that are still sepia-coloured in pale sunshine. On the north slope of the valley, as I went up to the Rackenfords', the oaks in the pastures, still in small leaf, had the lovely, arrested air of spring, as though time stood still for me.

Cicely was in her shadowy, flagged kitchen overlooking a yard enclosed by granite buildings. There are plenty of cob houses closer to the Moor than the Rackenfords' farm, and hardly a gatepost that is not granite in the surrounding country, but this farm, wholly grey, is an outpost of Dartmoor; and Cicely, wearing a white apron and black felt hat, indoors and out, seems to belong to a more formal and isolated community than mine. A bowl of cream scalded on the stove, two closed apple tarts were cooling on the table, a knife thrust under each, between the pastry and the tin. 'Robert's a master eater,' she said.

I asked after the family: her son Robert, who farms the land with the help of Nancy's husband; Anne and Mary, married and away. Her husband is dead.

Robert was cutting, she said, and had not come in last night till 'twas dimsy, and she was proper wicked. She talks, almost unchanged, the Devon of her youth, using words apparently harvested from the heavy soil, giving everything a gender. Anne's house had been broken into while she was at market, 'When er went to the liddle window 'e were open.' Mary had been to a family wedding. 'One of the bridesmaids were light and small'—on the family side. 'The other were stuggy.'

I told her what the doctor had said to me.

She raised her pale, serene face, the musing face of someone who works alone, unpractised in the expressions of sociability, and as feeling flowed into channels uncluttered with rubbish her look expressed all the sympathy that was necessary. Her way of speaking was typical of one who uses words as though they were precious grain, weighed and distributed carefully.

''Tis lucky you'm educated, Lucy.'

'Why in the world?'

'You'll have your thoughts,' she said. 'I ain't mazed about book-learning, myself. 'Tidn' much use to folks who can work. But for them as can't, 'tis a standby.'

She bent to her cooking again. Presently she asked whether

I had seen Pamela. I told her, not yet; I thought I'd go in on my way home.

'Er'll have some suggestions to make,' she said. 'Pamela knows her own mind; there's no widdle-waddle with she. Though er don't do the drapers no gude,' she added.

I laughed. Pamela and her husband appear to share the same wardrobe—if it can be called that—of shirts and trousers and gumboots.

Cicely continued, balancing between severity and amusement, 'It marvels me. Drapers would be out of business if us all went about like she.'

Long before the point where the Vicarage drive shakes off its mantle of shrubs and sweeps round the bend discreetly hiding the square stone front of the house, I could hear, on my way to find Pamela, two voices raised in determined, unrancorous argument.

'I want to be Ariel.'

'Well, you can't.'

'Why not?'

'Because I'm going to be Lady Macbeth.'

Somewhere between wiliness and conciliation the first retorted: 'How about me being Ariel if you're the Bosun?'

On the lawn Peter and Simon sprawled before identical books. 'Hallo, Luce,' they said.

I answered in their own abbreviations. 'Hallo Pete. Hallo Si. What are you doing at home today?'

'Half term,' Peter replied. 'Jodge is home, too.'

On a smaller, equally unkempt lawn nearer the house, George was parading a month-old calf on a halter round what I guessed to be a ring of imaginary buyers. His brothers tried shortening his name to Geo, for a time, but finding that they were calling him Joe, in search of accuracy changed it to Jodge, and the placid, rustic sound of it suits well the only true farmer of the three.

'Come to see Mother?' Simon looked up from the Shakespeare he had been hurrying through. With the book open at *The Tempest*, his face, with the fair, untidy fringe and blue eyes almost exactly duplicated by his brothers', wore the satisfied and expectant look of one who has placed himself in a good position for the start of a race.

'Yes,' I said.

'She's indoors, cooking.'

When I crossed the small lawn George was standing with the calf thoughtfully blowing his knees. In his hand was an imaginary catalogue. 'Now, Gentlemen,' he was saying, 'what'll you give me for this beautiful cow? She has a good, square, hard-wearing bag, and she'll grow into money. 'Lo, Luce,' he called. 'What d'you think of Olivia?'

'There's a dairy for you,' I said. 'She'll pay you over and over again. Look at her vessel, Gentlemen,' imitating the same auctioneer as he. 'A sweet and gracious cow, from an honest herd.'

As I walked through the house, an open door revealed the drawing-room with model railway lines laid out on the bare boards where once the pattern of a worn, rose-coloured carpet lost itself beneath rosewood and walnut furniture. I passed the Doctor's old study—its carpeted, overcrowded comfort replaced by a kitchen chair on a bare floor, and a table piled with bills and account books and milk recording sheets—and the dining-room, carpetless, with kitchen chairs and a battered packing case or two filling the places of Hepplewhite chairs that have disappeared, unregretted, with the rest of the furniture, to improve a milking herd.

Pamela was in the kitchen, tumbling things into saucepans and splashing the contents of the saucepans over an old black range. 'It's this grinding domesticity that gets me down,' she mourned from a cloud of steam.

She had evidently come in from the fields, as always at the last minute. Wearing a torn shirt and patched cord trousers of her husband's, her skin browned and hair bleached by the sun, she would have looked like a fair gypsy if she had worn a skirt, and as out of place in a kitchen, if the kitchen had retained the order once natural to it. But gumboots littered the verges of the thoroughfares between range and sink, the larder and table; pots and pans overflowed the crowded sink;

clothes, once aired by the fire, cluttered the dresser among newspapers and books that no one ever seems to put away; three or four sacks, spread at different times inside the door for a mat, had joined the boots with the odd bits of rubbish, briefly treasured, that children bring in from the fields. Yet there is something more subtle about this room than mere untidiness; some vague emanation that is the opposite of the buttressed exclusion of the weather, the fields and the yard, essential to Cicely's kitchen and, once, to my mother's: as though here the very walls were thinner, and attention directed all the time not inwards but outside.

I began washing the breakfast things, which were still on the table, and returning them to the table for dinner, while I knew that Pamela waited for me to tell her the specialist's verdict, making more clatter than usual over her hateful tasks, urging herself on, 'Tom'll be in any minute, clamouring for food.'

When I told her, 'I've thought, continually, about it, in case it should come to something like this,' she said, 'and I don't expect it's much use my telling you how sorry I am. But you will be able to carry on, won't you? You know your farm blindfolded already.' She added, doubtfully for her, 'There's one thing you can do: you can write down everything you see or remember, to fix it in your mind. I'll read it to you later, if you like. You used to be mad on writing things down when you were a kid.' Then honesty forced her to speak her mind. 'It beats me how so many people who're keen on the country seem to spend half the time they might be raising something merely scribbling about it.'

I told her I had thought of it, and had begun, tentatively; and I told her the curious discovery I have made already: that it is as though I saw everything for the first time, instead of almost the last; how people saunter in with all their life-known habits newly displayed, as though they were new acquaintances, and conclusions that have slowly ripened in a lifetime of half-realized observation suddenly spring into mind as discoveries. Then we laughed about Cicely's views on education, and her promise of Pamela having ideas. 'She didn't expect me to have any, you notice,' I said. 'You can't make a silk purse out of a sow's ear.'

Pamela banged a saucepanful of potatoes on to the hottest part of the stove. 'Who the hell wants a silk purse, anyway?' she asked disgustedly. 'Except, of course, to sell.'

'And I thought that were just a leedle bit covetous,' said Dick. He cast about for a word equal to the strength of his feelings. One, in fact, that took more saying. 'Ah, I thought that were just a leedle bit coveteous.'

'What was, Dick?' He was eating his lunch on a corner of the kitchen table while I prepared dinner for my father and him and myself; for he still holds to the old-fashioned farm worker's habit of coming into the kitchen in the middle of the morning to eat his lunch of bread and cheese and tea. At seven in the morning he has a solitary bowl of bread and milk in his cottage, his dew-bit, and with his second meal he likes to expand in conversation.

'Why, making me take the donkey-trap a couple o' miles, evenings, to fetch spring water for Missis to wash the butter in or something.' He returned willingly to the beginning of his story. ''Tis sixty-three year since I first went to plough, and my hands would only just reach the handles. Liddle nipper o' ten, I were, but I had my own team, and I ploughed all day between two waggoners. They had a plough each side o' me, and I had to keep up with they. Half a crown a week Maister paid me, and at the end o' the day I used to take the liddle donkey trap to fetch water in a churn. Reckon they paid me my half crown for that, an' I ploughed for nothing.'

He raised his hand to brush the crumbs off the table, and thought better of it—a concession to my diminishing sight. While my father is ever on his guard against tricks of circumstance, experience has taught Dick broadminded suspicion of his fellow men, particularly his employers. They have always controlled his life, and he gets his own back by small acts of comfortable indulgence and private defiance; but whereas, in the past, he would quietly have swept his crumbs to the floor when I was not looking, now he evidently scorned to, because he thought that already I had no chance of seeing.

'Were you big for your age, at ten, Dick?' I asked. In his seventies the fine frame that was his pride in young manhood has become frail and angular, and his gait, formed in childhood between furrows, stiff jointed. But once he touched six foot four, with strength in proportion.

'No, proper liddle un, I were,' he said. 'Arms like two flails. And what d'you expect? There weren't much room when I were young, with sixteen of us, an' only a five-roomed cottage, an' not too much to eat, either, 'less you cut a bit of bacon off the side that hung in the passage, an' runned upstairs with it, an' cooked un outside, after.' He took his pipe from his pocket, and bent, surreptitiously, to knock out the dottle against the table leg before filling it, but changed his mind and went over to the window.

'I've bolted up they stairs, times,' he said. 'They were the second lot, because ours were once two cottages; the others went down to the kitchen. When I were fifteen or so I took to a bit o' poaching, an' one night I come home late, an' being very cold I sot on a chair by the hot ashes o' the fire. 'Twere so cold I pulled my jacket up over me 'aid an' falled asleep. Well, I were no sooner asleep than me feet went out an' knocked over the fender. Next thing I knowed, Mother'd come downstairs with a candle an' were hollering: "Faither, Faither, come quick. There's a man setting here with no 'aid!" While er peered upstairs for Faither, I raced across the passage an' up they second stairs. An' even now,' he concluded, 'there's volks as'll tell ee that cottage be haunted.'

He sat down to smoke his pipe comfortably on the window-seat. Hours mean nothing to Dick any longer. He has worked for my father since the end of the nineteen-fourteen war, and since he has retired and taken the old age pension, he continues to come to work for the two pounds a week that are all that the regulations allow, which at the rate for casual labour gives him nearly thirteen hours a week; and as he comes in to dinner almost every day, it is pretended by us all that he spreads his work over six days. Times, as he would say, in winter, when there is nothing for him to do but the jobs he finishes early in the week, I have seen his stilted figure cross the yard, a sack over shoulders bent against the slanting December rain, an hour before dinner—in time for me to put a few extra potatoes round the joint. In winter he wears a scarf of blue and grey check inside the neck of his tweed jacket weathered to the colour of dry slate, and turns the collar up with the lapels crossed and fixed with a large safety-pin on his chest. Under the knees of his cord trousers he wears garters of string, which hitch them up so that his ankles look very long and his feet enormous. Stalking across the yard on his invented errand, bent forward against the rain, he looks like a wading bird.

From his place by the window he watched my preparations for dinner with the detached yet affectionate stare of a cat, distantly approving of the apple tart that I finished and took out to the back kitchen to bake in the range—my mother's innovation, supplanting the old bread oven, and the bottlejack roasting oven that once stood in front of the open hearth.

'What was your mother like, Dick?' I asked, when I came back. I have heard all his stories over and over again, yet, in each telling, as his memory fastens on some detail, a shaft of light may discover some forgotten portrait or miniature landscape that I have never seen.

He took his short pipe out of his mouth, and replied in his soft voice, 'Er'd a bosom like a barrel and used to wear a hat, for best, with a liddle feather in front.'

He readily talks about his mother, whom he feared and loved; for he was born to be ruled by women, and to retaliate by privately hoodwinking them and referring to them always in terms of the highest admiration. He boasts of her position in the village, where the benefit of her own numerous experience was shared at every difficult confinement, and her universal efficiency called upon at every sick-bed and in the performance of Last Offices. 'She were there,' he says, 'whenever a chiel were born; and whenever anyone died, 'twas her they sent for to do the last. There were nothing shoddy about anything she done.' When he was thirty he extended his inexhaustible capacity for admiration to include Rose, his wife. She had succeeded to his mother's amateur position in the professional one of District Nurse, dragging the reins from his mother's unwilling fingers. 'My Missis,' he says, 'were *the* person in the village.'

Dick on the window-seat looked like his father. He still had on the scorched panama hat which he wears, like my father, for corn harvest and haymaking. If he had come in with my father he would have followed his example and taken it off. As it was, he had forgotten it, for from habit he would as soon have thought of removing it as his waistcoat. At all other times of year he wears a cap, weathered and moulded to the contours of his bony head, but sporting all summer a flower from his garden tucked above one corner of the peak, and all winter a Flanders poppy.

Dick's father used to come up to the farm for haymaking and corn harvest as all the other old men went to the other farms, invited or not, to advise on the building of the ricks. A lifetime's experience, backing a glance, told them the size of the crop, then stiffly they paced out the dimensions of the rickbeds, and with reedy, indignant voices defended their decision, which no one seriously challenged. If they were active enough they helped to build the ricks, standing on the growing fabric with a pitchfork to distribute the hay, or kneeling to grasp sheaves of corn by the twine, placing them heavily, the ears laid inwards, jealously watching the squared sides of the hayricks, or the circumference, tapering downwards, of beehive ricks of corn.

Their timeless garments were almost indistinguishable from those Dick wears now; only, perhaps, their trousers of hard, dark cloth or corduroy gartered below the knee with string or leather, were a little narrower. Their shirts of flannel, or thick, unyielding cotton material, broad-banded with faded stripes once red and blue and grey, collarless, with a stud in the front of the collarband; their waistcoats, which they kept on, however hot the sun; their straw hats the colour of toast; all seem to me to be as like Dick's clothes as his face and frame and gestures are like his father's.

I have almost forgotten the father's face, in contemplation of the son's; but the bumpy nose and rounded brows, the blue eyes and high cheekbones, the narrow chin which seems as though it will run to a point, then is suddenly squared off, the character mapped in lines of humour and shrewdness and obstinacy—the family face—is the face of a farm worker, rather than a farmer, a man of no property beyond his skill and endurance and opinions; and its contours have been generations in the making.

Perhaps Dick's face is less rugged than his father's; with his sons the family face has become almost urbane. Easier living has softened its features; education and their mother's professional background have made them less—local. With them the old Devon speech, like calm water softly lapping on a shore: 'Did ee putt un *een,* then?' 'Ah, I putt un *een,* but er got out agin'—the fall and rise and fall—has been levelled out. They do not make music of vowels, or improvise words to suit the moment, as Dick, who describes a soft, ungainly lump as a wallage, or use time-honoured improvisations like 'apple dranes' for wasps. They do not say 'proper wicked' for angry, 'terrify' for tease, 'ignorant' for ill-mannered, or 'mazed' for mad. Rose was a strict mother.

Dick met his future wife in nineteen-nine. 'I zeed Missis, first, when she were trying to move old Bill Yeo. Twenty stone er weighed, an' she were washing of un. "Come in and help me," er called through the windy. In I went, an' there 'twas.'

Since he first went to plough he had worked on various farms, his height and strength increasing. He never stayed in one place for long, but wherever there was heavy work to be done he was wanted; and in time of difficulty, such as the bogging down of a loaded harvest cart or a thrashing machine, he was sent for. A landless John Ridd in strength, his reward was abundant honour, and cider. 'I've drunk enough to float a battleship, or sink un. I can't remember which,' he says, remembering an old compliment.

His marriage with Rose was a surprise to the village, for his talent for floating battleships and his great strength were his only assets, and the nurse had been smiled at for keeping herself to herself. But she became Nurse Meldon, and she wore her title like Royalty, with her consort, not even boasting plain Mister, seeming to walk always a pace behind her. Sometimes I used to meet them in the lane, when I was a child—Sunday was the only day one would see them together —Nurse would be leading the youngest by the hand: Mary, her hair freshly out of curl-papers, whom everyone would stop to admire; while Dick, as usual, walked a step behind, followed by three dishevelled little boys: Edward, Albert and Henry.

Dick continued to float battleships. When he first came to us my mother demurred when he was called away to a trial of strength, leaving all our work to my father. But my father, with his customary pursing of the lips before he expressed an opinion, said: 'If I employed the sexton he'd be called away to dig graves.' Dick was always away until at least the middle of the following day, for he dared not come back to the village and earshot of Nurse until he had recovered from the effect of his reward.

He used, in those days, to tell me stories of his boyhood under the thatch where the other fifteen little Meldons were bred. Perhaps Nurse and his own children were not interested. He served with the Devonshire Regiment during the first war, but he never spoke of his soldiering days, even when the memory was green; his acute observation never seems to have focused on surroundings so detached from familiar association, and his imagination passed them by.

'Where did you come in the family?' I used to ask him, to get him going.

'Can't remember,' he said easily, 'thirteenth, I think. Tell ee what, though,' he continued, with one of his illuminating afterthoughts, 'I never had a hot dinner till I were seven. Time Mother'd given the older ones theirs, what were left were cold. When I were seven, some o' the big uns had left home. Course, three more liddle uns come along, but by then I were more advanced in the family, like.'

I asked him whether they were ever all at home together.

'Times,' he said, 'then us had a huge table in the garden, and all ate there.'

When he was five he went to school, to the care first of a lady infant-teacher, then of the black-bearded schoolmaster. With the first he behaved quite well, his respect for authoritative women governing him; but on promotion to the master's teaching he decided against book-learning, and began playing truant. He found it paid, for when the master started sending a boy to find him, someone had the idea of offering Dick a penny to stay away on condition that he kept the chase going for the whole morning.

The day of reckoning came, of course. At the end of one sunny morning Dick and his pursuer arrived at school to find the master, cane in hand, ready to give Dick a beating. Dick had no conventional ideas about deferring to authority; he fought as a man might on the scaffold, and with the method of a terrier. He fastened his grip and hung on.

When justice had been done the school was dismissed, and when the children returned in the afternoon they found their master beardless. In the struggle Dick had torn out a fistful, and the rest had been painfully shaved off during dinner time.

'What were you christened, Dick?' I once asked him. I expected that his parents would have run short of names when they had already thought of a dozen; but I underestimated them.

'Richard William Thomas,' he replied.

'You didn't name any of your children after you then?'

He considered me reproachfully. 'They were all named after the Royal Family,' he said. 'Missis wouldn't consider nothing else, course.'

Now Nurse Meldon has been dead for two years, and Dick

'does' for himself in the cottage where they raised their royally named brood.

When I had prepared dinner I went out to help turn the hay by hand. The swath-turner had broken down.

My father and Dick were already working rhythmically along the lines of gleaming swaths that patterned the field in diminishing squares, throwing abroad the undergrass with the methodical, sparing gestures of old men. I picked up a wooden rake and began.

Dick drew level with me, turning a neighbouring swath. Before I began to listen, he had advanced in a conversation he had had the night before with a visitor at the Tenor Bell. 'Old vashioned, er thought I were. "What did you have to eat, when you were young?" er zaid. Ask questions for a pastime, they foreigners. "Bread an' cheese," I zaid. Er zaid that Dorset way they called the cheese Blue Vinney, or something. "What did you call *your* cheese?" er zaid. "What did us call it?" ' Dick's voice rose in exasperation, in spite of stooping over the hay. ' "Why, us called it cheese!" '

Although he talked all the time, he drew ahead of me, and so that we should be level again he turned a few yards of my swath over, glancing defensively under the brim of his hat at my father working steadily on the other side of the field.

Every time we paused to straighten our stiffening backs the hedges faced us brilliantly, showered with dog roses, their weight pulling the sprays downwards in garlands of flushed flowers. Dick's conversation rose and fell like the breathing of a dreamer. The familiar beauty of our surroundings—repetition of a lifetime's hay harvests—did not interrupt his thoughts. He had embarked on a talk about cremation. 'I wouldn't 'ave had my Missis burnt. 'Pon me zoul, if I'd thought they were burning she I'd a gone mazed. After all er'd done for me and the kids er didn't deserve it.'

The field, where we had turned it, was still patterned with lines of swaths; but now they were tumbled, the grasses silvering in the sunshine, the flowers faded. When grasses fall under the mower they all lie in one direction, so that the top layer protects the swaths like a thatch. It is after turning, that hay, tousled and unprotected, suffers in the rain. Our morning's work had made it vulnerable.

Vulnerable. The word that had suggested itself when I was talking to Nancy a day or two ago came back to rest on me. The elms in the hedges moved lightly, the leaves seeming blue against the blue sky. House-martins flew high, creamy breasted, purring and twittering. It was perfect weather for saving the hay. I closed my eyes, and in the same moment looked forward and back, at trees in hedges and pasture in small leaf again, misted with a colour not yet green, but a subtle underwater colour of green and brown, sunlight netted in branches so that they seemed to be hung with pearls, the jutting twigs of oak and delicate angled elm clear against the sky: the spring's renewal that I shall not see again.

As we walked back to the house for dinner, Dick drew a piece of paper out of his waistcoat pocket. 'I've ordered Missis's 'aidstone,' he said. 'Would you like to see the words?' He began to pass it to me, but changed his mind because he thinks I can no longer read. 'No, course,' he said. 'I'll read it to ee.'

Seeming to read, he recited, with pauses between the lines:

Here lies
Rose Meldon
Beloved Wife of
Dick.

4

The Judge and Mrs Mowbray sat, one on each side of the fireplace, she in an old-fashioned black coat and skirt vaguely suggesting a riding habit, and a hat with a diamond brooch pinned in the brim, still wearing the memory of beauty; he, frail and diminished but, like a sinking fire, capable of unexpected sparks and little flashes of energy. They were sitting in silence, not having heard the clamour of the dogs in the drive; and I thought, as often before in that room of muted colours, of winter trees, their sap stilled in a grey sleep in the sun, folded in the laced shadows of their branches, bearing no leaves of last year, no buds of this.

Mrs Mowbray had telephoned to ask me to tea, and I had been met, as always, by a couple of silent and dignified old foxhounds following the pack of terriers whose clangour dispenses with the need for a front door bell. Mr Silvester, who, with his wife, rules a master and mistress even older than themselves, let me in and led me softly to the drawing-room, making something professional of the short journey.

The Judge rose stiffly and slowly to his feet, gripping the arms of his chair with pale hands, but sank, suddenly, back into it.

'Oh John, dear, whatever are you doing, dearest?'

Mrs Mowbray was sympathetic and at the same time faintly triumphant. They have, towards one another, the protective and competitive bearing of lifelong companions who have grown very old together.

'Lucy, dear,' she said, when the Judge had assured her patiently, and with studied surprise, that nothing was wrong, 'I want to talk to you.'

I drew my chair close to hers. Mrs Silvester is the only one in the house who stoops to the use of a hearing aid.

The Judge sat upright in his chair again. 'Where has Silvester gone?' he asked.

'What did he say?' asked Mrs Mowbray.

I told her; and she replied, loudly, that he had gone to fetch the tea.

'What's that?' said the Judge.

'What did he say?' asked Mrs Mowbray. 'It's all right,' she answered him soothingly, when I had told her, 'you can't hear.'

'I can hear you perfectly, my dear,' replied the old man, unexpectedly.

Mr Silvester brought in a tray, and while Mrs Mowbray poured almost invisible tea from a silver pot, and we nibbled Mrs Silvester's wafer sandwiches and miniature iced cakes, the Judge told us about alterations to a friend's garden, counties away, as though it adjoined his own. It is one of the Mowbrays' singularities to talk about their friends' houses as though the intervening country and its population did not exist.

On a faded rosewood table, out of reach of the dogs, who had come in with Mr Silvester and sat gimleting us with their attention, a cat was eating cake, noisily and crumbily.

'Lucy,' said Mrs Mowbray—the Judge had relapsed into silence, breathing light and fast, his face faintly blue—'you must learn Braille. John, dear,' she shouted, 'who was it taught Amy to read Braille so beautifully?'

The Judge roused himself and leant forward again. 'Amy?' he said. 'Charlie's girl? She married one of Julian's boys, the youngest.'

'Yes. Yes. I know that,' Mrs Mowbray retorted. 'I want to know who taught her Braille. You won't remember.'

'I remember quite well,' he said, composedly. 'It was Dr Ivy Williams.'

'Of course,' said Mrs Mowbray. 'Why didn't you say so at once? We must see whether she will teach Lucy.'

Mr Silvester came to collect the tea things while I was leaving. His glance fell reprovingly on the crumbs which the cat had left on the table.

'Will you be giving the cat a saucer of milk, Madam?' he asked; and he put his hand behind his ear to catch the reply.

Mrs Mowbray gave him a defiant look. 'My cat only drinks out of the jug. You know that as well as I do, Silvester,' she said.

In the urgency of the past few days, grasping only the imperious necessity to take a last look round, I have taken no account of the obvious fact that soon printed books will be closed for me. Richard was an avid reader until he became a farmer, reading with undistracted absorption. It is the townsman's luxury, we used to say later, that absence of distraction by the endless diversity of the open air, by the instant of beauty or experience that might be missed. After he came to live with us he had, like me, little time for reading; and on winter evenings, after we were married—the long winter evenings that farm people speak of lovingly in summer, which, when they come, are never long enough—satisfied by the day's work and the fulfilling variety of days, we drowsily returned, for the most part, to books we already knew. But always, ahead of us, was some imaginary time of infinite leisure to read, so, in the time we had, we read about books; and the notices in papers gave us a nodding acquaintance with them. It was like being among a crowd where you know only a few people intimately, but you know who most of them are: the comfortable companionship one finds at a show or a sale.

5

Father has the old haylift out: a pole with cross-beam and ropes and pulleys and the wide-jawed iron grip for lifting huge bulks of hay from the ground to the top of the growing rick, dwarfed by the mast, a branchless tree. Soon after I was born he bought it for four pounds ten in a sale, and every year, when it comes out of the barn, its rigging transforms the blue skies and light airs of haytime into seaside weather.

Archie Wrangways works on the rick, bending to spread the hay which the grip lifts up to him, leaning on his fork and brushing sweat off his forehead with a sun-blackened forearm while he waits for Dick to guide down the grip with a rope, and load it, opening the iron jaws and closing them on their burden. Father, on the tractor, hauls the line which draws up the loaded grip, and when Archie shouts from the top, Dick, who still has the lead from the grip in his hand, jerks it, and the jaws open and the load is dropped. After a moment of leisure and comment Dick pulls on the lead again while Father drives the tractor towards the rick, paying out the line, and the even chain of the work is repeated. Jim has been lent by the Rackenfords in return for help we shall give them later, and brings the hay in from the field with a buckrake and borrowed tractor. All work gaily under the bright sky and light wind. Only when Dick sends up an extra large gripful Archie gives him a reproachful look. There is a festive, harvest atmosphere. Everyone passing in the lane comes into the field to see how we are getting on.

Mrs Shenley, the pretty wife of a gentleman farmer, stopped her car on her morning shopping journey and came in to speak to Father, who immediately stopped the tractor and brought the work to a standstill.

'You have some good hay, this year,' she said professionally.

'Ah,' said Father, who expands from his usual reserve into gallantry only for her, ''tis gude enough. 'Twould be better if us were alone.'

'Oh, why?' she asked innocently, as she did last year, and the year before.

'They do say,' said Father, talking broad for effect, 'that the only way to be certain of a gude rick is to take a handful of hay out of it, kiss a pretty woman and brush her cheeks with the hay, then put it back.'

'Really,' said Mrs Shenley, adding, reprovingly, 'you've stopped the work, talking to me, Mr Belstone.'

'Ah,' Father said, with affected concern, ''tis a pity, for I'm key-man here. I always take the key job, so that I know how badly 'tis done.' Before starting the tractor again he waited for her answer, which he knew would come.

Wrinkling her pretty nose, she replied, severely, 'I think the master should be able to do every job better than anyone else.'

With a satisfied expression Father went on with his work. It always happens: he draws her into making the pawky observations which he might make himself, though with more wit, and delights in their absurd incongruity with her charming face.

Tom came past, driving his cows through the Vicarage gate to a field down the lane.

'He do drive they cows too fast,' Archie remarked from his observation point.

''Tidn' that er drives em too fast,' said Dick, thoughtfully, leaving the grip lying idle while he straightened his back to look.

'Ah?' said Archie, on an inviting note of interrogation; he stuck the thumb of his spare hand into the armhole of his waistcoat and widened his stance comfortably, leaning on his fork.

'Well,' Dick said, 'er do seem always in a hurry, doing extry things wi' his arms an' legs, like, only er don' get along any faster'n us.'

Archie tilted his hat back and drew his arm meditatively across his brow. 'What causes it, d'you think?'

Dick brought out his pipe and considered filling it, looked at Father, who was combing the sides of the rick with a rake, and changed his mind. 'Education,' he said, and bent to his work again.

Like the other gentry, the farmers who Father says can raise nothing but their hats, Tom's movements allow an expenditure of energy unhampered by the economy learnt during boyhood while carrying out a day's work to its end. And there is another difference, a demeanour of bustling activity quite opposed to Father's cautious gestures: Tom is always mastering the land, fighting it. The slow advance of the seasons that sweeps Father in its course meets Tom forestalling it, disciplining it, striding ahead and defying it.

Shouting cheerful insults to his plodding herd, he disappeared round the bend in the lane, and Dick and Archie exchanged comments which were drowned by the noise of the tractor. All the men like Tom, and all offer him age-old advice, with falsely modest expressions, which he waves aside in favour of new strategies for winning his battle with the soil.

Richard was not born on the land, either; he was a townsman, and he, in another way, was unlike a farmer bred: there was a difference which showed in his gift for seeing things, always, as if for the first time. He never saw the country, the real country, until he was ten, when his parents brought him for a holiday to discover the county of forbears who had passed on a Devon name, Shebbear. Going into the lane one day to post a letter, my mother found them watching the cows loafing in for milking, and touched by their interest she asked the strangers in to tea.

It is impossible to balance the picture of a child, seen by a child, with the remembrance of a grown man. My childish judgement was narrow, and prejudiced by adult conversation overheard, idealized by storybooks, based on small experience; and I saw a funny little boy, a town boy in town clothes, pale, and, I was quite sure, timid. In what I believed would be my father's opinion, I said to myself 'a proper little nestle-tripe', the name given, in my mother tongue, to the smallest of a litter of pigs. His hair was no particular colour, darkened by much hair oil, his eyes were brown, and he was, by our standards, puny. Only his eyes and his expression, alert and kind, remained the same when his character had filled out and I grew adult enough to discern it.

Everyone was a little larger than life during tea. The visitors were impressed by the spread: the ham and homemade bread and butter, the apple tart and cream and cakes, and my family grew almost boisterously hearty, my mother saying, more often than was necessary, 'There's nothing boughten in this house.' Richard's parents expanded and began to talk loudly, jovially, as people often do when they visit farms, and to boast that they came of farming stock. When they stood up I noticed that the father straddled a bit in his blue, town suit. They were getting on well, and presently, the better to enjoy one another's company, they told me to take Richard out into the fields. When we were in the yard I told him, no doubt to show off, that we would take the ferret with us.

The harvest was done, and we crossed the stubble in the characteristic evening stillness of late summer; heavy quiet, as pervasive as weather, intensified by a distant, receding train, a faraway milker calling in his cows. Richard stayed close to me, like a town dog in the country.

'D'you like it here?' I asked him patronizingly.

'Yes,' he replied, coldly. 'I do, if you really want to know. It's only that down our way you don't have to listen, you just hear everything, like buses and trams and kids yelling.'

Probably I made some snubbing retort. He had hit on the temper of the hour with uncomfortable precision; and now, if I am in that place when the tide of the day is running out, the recollection of that evening brushes the edge of memory, not as a procession of events, but whole and instantaneous.

The bank at the end of the stubble was, and is still, a vaulted burrow, hollowed out by generations of rabbits, with many entrances where roots of oak and ash and sallow grope for a lost hold in red earth. I arranged the nets over one or two holes, still showing off and without any intention of catching rabbits which I would not have thought of killing by myself. But I placed the nets with a great display of craftiness, to show that it was not a thing any fool could do, fixing the top corner to a peg, spreading the sides with maddening care, laying the bottom corner in the burrow. Then I opened the ferret's bag, and she crept out with her curious, halting gait, arching and extending her body that was the colour of washleather; sensitive, fastidious and savage. Richard was more aghast, even, than I had anticipated, and as he backed away she looped after him, weaving with her head, gazing upwards with her short-sighted, unblinking, red-opal eyes, chattering with a sound like smothered laughter.

'Will she bite?' he asked.

'You bet,' I said.

I picked her up airily, taking care to grasp her safely behind the jaws, and put her in the mouth of a hole which she crept into, dragging her tail. Immediately, a rabbit bolted into one of the nets and rolled down the bank and lay rigid at the bottom, the net pressing a honeycomb pattern on its fur, its eyes protruding and shining with fear. Knowing that Richard would not suspect that what I did was unusual, and prepared, if necessary, to give some fanciful explanation, I set it free, and it hastened across the corner of the field to the cover of another bank, kicking up its heels and its white scut in a lighthearted salute as it reached safety.

'Good for him,' Richard said. And I decided that he was no sporting man.

The ferret reappeared, nose working, head prying from side to side. She crept along the terraced paths trodden by rabbits, looping her body along, and always moving. She followed the tented alleys in the long, yellowing grass of the bank's side, the tracks worn down by animals that live in a hedge bottom, under pavilions of reddening brambles, and disappeared down a hole. At once the thumping sound of a fight followed: she was hunting on her own account. When she reappeared at the mouth of the burrow she backed and disappeared when she saw me. When, at last, I caught her, she gave a stuttering cry of anger. Richard, I thought, was being given a fine display of my prowess. But after her entry into another hole we heard the muffled cries of a rabbit, then silence. She had killed, and there she was likely to stay, making a meal of her prey and, very possibly, sleeping it off.

By this time I discovered, surprised, that the sun had gone down, and mist folded distant fields until the boundary of our world was our own trees and hedges. As we went back to the yard for a spade to dig the ferret out, owls began to call from invisible trees, and the white owl that lived in the implement shed killed in the rickyard and gave a shriek, like a finger drawn down a shutter, that stirred the skin beneath my hair. Perhaps Richard's hair oil denied him this not unpleasing sensation; his whole frame shuddered.

We were glad to reach lamplight and the warmth of the sitting-room where our parents were thoroughly enjoying themselves, and, by this time, knew a good deal about one another. Richard's father, I found afterwards, was a laboratory assistant at a London hospital, the trusted lab. man of some professor. 'We scientists' he was saying, from an authoritative stance on the hearth; but I see, now, that though the expression became a family joke, he was a scientist in the word's truest sense, in spite of his comic little tricks of self-glorification and obvious imitations of his master: for from him Richard learnt his searching discontent with the surface of things, and increased the gift to a talent for seeing things always new, which he shared with me in unknowing preparation for what now lies ahead.

After we had been in the room a moment my mother asked me to shut up her fowls for her, and I went out, intending to come back and enjoy a little of the adult comedy before taking a lantern and spade to fetch the ferret; but when I came back I found that Richard had disappeared, and before I set off he came into the room with the ferret grasped with both hands, like a child presenting flowers at the opening of a fête. His hands were scored with marks of her resentment, and he need not, really, have held her so firmly, for her teeth were closed tightly on one of his thumbs. Father released him, and he explained that he had found the ferret out in the open, on the bank.

He slid away from the grown-ups.

'Weren't you afraid of the owls?' I said.

Someone asked, at the same moment, 'Weren't you afraid of the dark?'

'No,' he said, 'it was wolves I was frightened of.'

Everyone else thought that superbly funny, but I saw nothing peculiar in it at all. In the world of imagination my discernment was clear enough: we all put what construction we may on our fears, and Richard had been walking in the jungle.

He came to the farm as a pupil after he left school, and stayed to be Father's right hand. We should have inherited the farm together, for at the moment when he brought the ferret in, though we did not recognize it, Dick might have said 'There 'twas.' We married four years before the War began.

Dick is dusting the kale field with Derris powder, dragging two sacks, nailed to a broomhead and partially filled with the powder, over the rough earth and the heads of the little plants so that the Derris works through the coarse meshes of the sacking. The method is as out of keeping with this age of mechanized farming as the old man's indifference to the time it takes. But the procedure is so simple—as fundamentally direct in conception as ploughing or breaking down a seedbed with a harrow—that if a cataclysm destroyed all memory of machinery, in time it would almost certainly be rediscovered; and while Dick trudges up and down the slowly whitening field he has a touch of the everlasting.

Once a scene like this emphasized the permanence of our way of getting a living; now it intensifies my sense of parting, with sharp reminders of the practical consequences of my vanishing sight.

I see myself preparing vegetables with a magnifying glass; groping and peering for something fallen on the floor, waiting for help; the once lightly accepted responsibility for keeping an eye on things lost for ever, and everything that once spared attention for the passing of the outdoor day done in slow time.

Worst of all, a thought too distasteful to be faced squarely, shall I be forced, at last, to hand over to another woman all but the polite semblance of managing the house, and the traditional occupations of the farm wife: the poultry and dairy work, the dependability to provide warmth and comfort and rise to sudden emergency? When feeling is uppermost in mind, the unspeculative eye is apt to settle on small objects with concentration which thoughtful observation blurs. The anxieties reflected by Dick's plodding figure must have driven my undirected attention on to the ground, for I saw for the first time how flowers of scarlet pimpernel, small disc faces open to the sun, disclosed a ring of cyclamen at the base of their brilliant petals, colours beloved of God, for cyclamen veins the underside of scarlet poppy petals, ringing them, where the stem joins the flower, with a circlet almost black. I picked a poppy on the headland, unaware that I was reaching Sanctuary, and discovered that the vivid, crumpled, silken flower lay cold in my hand, and suddenly I stood on the edge of a new world, an unexplored territory of touch and sound and intuition.

7

The rick is half finished and covered with a sheet, while the hay which should have completed it lies flat and lifeless in the shorn field, dark and matted, flecked with blackened clover leaves, covered with bright water drops. Slugs crawl over the unturned swaths, mud-coloured, leaving a trail of slime. On the headland Meadow Brown butterflies rise lazily from long, wet grasses and fly heavily over the dingy swaths.

From the south west the sky drives towards the house, covered with layer upon layer of cloud. Clouds stoop over the Moor, and the tors break into their surface and tear off ragged edges which hurry in tatters across the dark slopes. Then rain blots out the mass and the fields near it are hidden in mist which reaches the farm in soft, driving rain moving like thin smoke. Elms in the hedges toss and turn up their leaves, paling in the wind, leaning away from it, as though a distracted woman threw her apron over her face.

' "When I made a chiel I made un wi' two gude feet an' sense in 'is 'aid." ' Snug in the kitchen, Nancy knelt on the floor, turning out a cupboard, quoting her neighbours' conversation, while I made pastry.

'Who said that, Nancy?'

'Mr Wrangways,' she said.

'Do the others talk like that?' Fluting the edges of a batch of pasties, shaping the cool, resilient dough with a twist, learnt in childhood, of finger and thumb, and remembering that soon it would be done by touch alone, it was not difficult to sound preoccupied; for anything that sounds like attack sends Nancy flying to her neighbours' defence, and it is only when she is busy, and the thoughts uppermost in her mind bubble up in conversation, that she gives away their constant small persecution.

'Oh yes,' she said. 'Archie's no worse than the rest.'

'Do you mean Mr Willsworthy and Dick join in?'

'Oh yes,' she said, and added, because I was showing too much interest, 'they can't help of it.'

The women preserve a code of behaviour probably as old as village life, and enforce it with hints and sly digs, a word to a neighbour loud enough to be overheard, a cold shoulder expressed in elaborate charade. By such discordance in the comparative harmony of everyday life a village keeps its vitality and a good name; without it, one which should ideally be carefree and neighbourly becomes lax and unruly, until it collapses into no more than a ragged collection of dwellings.

On our village pleasure-ground of cock-shy criticism her father's eccentricities have placed Nancy as a target. If she had stayed single perhaps she would never have outlived her neighbours' magnanimity: while she was single they could afford to be sorry for her, but as soon as she behaved like an equal they felt bound to put her in her place, and her marriage with Jim discovered a spring of asperity hitherto untapped.

'What does Jim say about it?'

'I haven't told Jim about it,' she said proudly. "Twouldn't be no gude for him to speak to em anyway, would it, because where'd he begin? The whole village does it.' And again she added: 'They can't help of it,' and, for the agreement she considered obvious, insisted: 'can em?'

Perhaps she is right. Among the men there is a legacy of rough joking, handed on from a robust past, for which personal feelings and physical disadvantages supply the raw material.

Almost every evening Willy Twitchen sits in the bar of the

Tenor Bell. Some disorder of circulation has made him blue, almost black in the face, and incapable of working to pay for sufficient beer to obliterate the distress of his old age. So he has to buy his comfort with what amusement he provides; and his currency is his weakness for animals. No one bears him the slightest ill-will; maybe it is a rough disguise for softheartedness that makes the men demand payment in teasing; and if his chief tormentor and benefactor, Mr Luppett, comes in when Willy and the regulars have already settled down, some variation on an ancient theme is played which is anticipated by everyone, except, apparently, Willy.

'Evenin', Will,' Mr Luppett says. 'Here, is that clock right?' He pretends great surprise. 'I've been giving the cow a hiding. Didn't know it took so long. Took a stick to her and beggar me if I didn't give her a hiding.' He talks so fast that Willy cannot get a word in: about how she gives no milk until she has been beaten. No milk yesterday, but ten gallons today after a hiding. She is a Hampshire cow, he explains, and that is how they have to be treated.

At last Willy, unable to make himself heard, walks over to his old friend and enemy and sticks his shaking finger in his face; but by this time he is very nearly speechless with pent-up agitation, and he has to lug his voice out of the depths of his chest. 'You cruel beggar, you. I'll report you. Serving animals like that. Tied up, I suppose. Defenceless.'

'Don't get so hot, Will,' Mr Luppett says, in burlesque conciliation. 'Here, I'll give ee a drink, an' you can tell me what you'd do. She's a Hampshire cow, mind.'

Willy never refuses a drink.

'Now, I've treated you,' Mr Luppett says, presently. 'Tell me what you'd do.'

Willy wipes his mouth on the back of his hand. 'Two knobs of sugar in my hand. I'd give em to her. "Come on, my beauty," I'd say.' His voice, harsh and rough, is as strange to tenderness as his terrible appearance—blackened face and swollen nose and livid glare—and as he goes through the mime of giving sugar to the cow and gentling her, everyone laughs.

This is one variant of a tale the men have used to enliven a break in the harvest work, a rest in the sun leaning on a hoe, since I was a child. Each man has his own way of acting out the piece: Archie Wrangways, with his long nose and an expression that seems always on the verge of winking, whose feet, during a lifetime of trudging rough land, have learnt to slope upwards from the heel, so that with stiff ankles and knees he moves from the hips with the rolling gait of a jointed doll; old Dick, humorous and stoical, worn to a shell by work and hard weather, but still, as he says, a joky article; older Bill Willsworthy, hardly ever leaving his cottage now, where he sits with his frail hands stretched before the fire, his reflective face, with its thin fringe of grey hair, bent over the warmth, missing his horses. Once he was a large man, with a smooth, thinking face, dressed in a snuff-coloured jacket and breeches and clean leggings; now he is shrunk, wheezing over the fire, only his ears alert, like a dozing cat. If anyone comes to the door and asks his wife how he is, he breaks off his long reverie to tell them: 'I ain't much better.'

'I hate to see animals served bad.' 'I like to see folks treated proper.' Expressions like these are natural to all three. But they all laugh at Willy. They all torment Nancy, who accepts their criticism as inevitably as it is given.

Lightheartedly expressing herself in words of which the meaning has less importance than their pleasure to her ear, in the singing cadences of our local speech, she must appear, to a stranger, like any other country girl. Yet even her choice of extravagant words seems to derive from the predicament that, setting her apart, makes her a seeker rather than an assentor.

It is impossible to capture the quality that is essentially hers, for pinned down it makes her appear strange. Generations of casual observation have bequeathed her the awareness that anticipates the coming storm and the unexpected break in hard weather; that overcomes her cottage-bred fear of the dark, and sends her out to drive off the skulking fox terrifying the roosting hens into silence. Is it some sound among the leaves, some new breath in the wind, that forewarns her of the weather? the sight of a cat's fur rising on its spine, as it drowses by the fire, that warns her of the fox? Probably it is some such simple manifestation; but few notice it except Nancy.

8

On a rare morning when Dick did not come up to the farm the weather lifted. Nancy brought word that he had a cold, and Father and I turned the hay: thick swaths grown heavy with moisture, that must be turned with a fork to air the ugly, greenish-yellow undergrass.

Every farmer in the west country knows such hay harvests —the complement of halcyon days of blue skies and sailing clouds and wandering breezes—when the air is heavy, so heavy that it rests on the back of the haymaker throwing the hay left and right, tossing abroad the lurid, sweating undergrass. The sky is pearly and the sun invisible, yet the air is hot and bright and full of insects and horseflies that settle unfelt until they bite and raise a weal. The gaze fixes on the long swath charting a course across the field, the back stiffening, the eye straying in the boundless country of the mind until it is surprised by the unexpected: a buzzard's brindled feather, a murdered rabbit's brittle skull, then on. So Father and I moved over the field, like figures contained in a dream.

In the middle of the morning we rested against a bank at the top of the field and shared the tea and fruit-cake I had brought out. On the other side of the valley Mr Luppett's ricks of last year still stood untouched among the barnlike structures of the year before, a village of ricks, dwarfing the low, cob house.

'He do look to the future, Ern Luppett,' Father said drily. 'Proper collector, he be. Reckons to leave his hay to a museum, shouldn't wonder.'

The mid-morning train dawdled past.

'That used to go by when I were a boy—a minute or two earlier, of course.' His gaze followed the line back in the direction of the family farm, and I half expected that he might make some more direct reference to his disinheritance. When he and his brother Stephen come face to face, as they must from time to time at shows and sales, they stop briefly, to speak, both scorning any false show of joviality, yet held stiffly for a moment by the tie of kinship. Other farmers, speaking of one brother, must sometimes ask: 'Do you know the other?' Then, no doubt, some version of the family split follows. But no one, except my mother, has ever spoken about it to me. A private quarrel might have rebounded in reconciliation; but the beam of local limelight played on him by the terms of the old man's will, violating the fastidiousness that makes a virtue of the boast that we keep ourselves to ourselves, shrivelled my father into silence far more forbidding than a conflagration of anger.

The sun broke through, and in spite of the fact that a moment had passed when the family wasteland might have been opened up for cultivation we were very comfortable together. But as though the very tranquillity disturbed his foreboding mind into searching for some means of securing it, he broke out suddenly: 'Have you thought what we're going to do with the farm? I shan't live for ever, and I don't see how you'm going to carry on without me, now. Who'll you leave it to, anyway?'

'A museum?' I suggested, trying to entice him into the lightness of a short time ago; but he made no retort. He had drawn in his horns.

Nevertheless, I embarked on a project that has been in my mind ever since the day I knew my sight was failing. It was as good a moment as any.

'What about leaving it to Jim and Nancy? After all, Nancy's a relation of ours. Why not make Jim a partner now, and bring him in with us, then let them carry on?'

He parried, from habit, but so unhesitatingly that he might have had some such idea, himself. If he had been looking round for a young man to take his place he would certainly have thought of Jim, who matches his own back-to-the-wall doggedness with optimistic tenacity.

'They've got no children.'

'Nor have I, so we're no worse off than before.'

'What about Nancy's trouble?'

'Well, what about it? Harry wasn't really mad. You know that as well as I do.'

The argument warmed up, as usual, with a volley of blind shots.

'You can't fly in the face of Nature, to please yourself.'

'But you can invent a face for her, and defy anyone to fly in it.'

Seeing that we had both got our eye in, Father reached for a fork and waited for me to get up and go on with our work until he decided to bring up the subject again. But for once I did not stir, and instead tried out the effect of a surprise.

'Has it ever struck you that Nancy, and even poor old Willy Twitchen, lead lives in some ways more affluent than ours?' He made no reply, cautiously waiting to find out what was coming. 'I mean while we're always toiling away, saving up for a rainy day, for them it's more often rainy than not, and they knock off whatever they're doing and spend time on any prospect of happiness that comes their way.'

Father joyfully misunderstood me. 'So you'm thinking of having Will Twitchen to live with us, too?'

The words were shaped in a grimace, as he sampled the idea of sharing our kitchen with Willy, who, we both know, will never desert the shelter of his own broken-backed thatch. Living rough, sleeping rough, and smelling somewhat rough in the foggy warmth of the fire that simmers his scrappy meals, carefully sustaining the remnant of health that preserves his condemned cottage from the demolition that the Council has ordered on his departure, he engages in a static tug-of-war with the authorities who would like to remove him to the sterile comfort of an old people's home. Half agreeing, then forgetting, not understanding and retiring into silence, he keeps the contest stationary on a worn-out patch of ground, alternately protesting that he was 'brung up there', and will never leave until he's screwed down, then playing with the idea of three square meals a day and a warm bed under a good roof.

I took up my fork, then. It was the moment for leaving the conversation for serialization later. But it reached its conclusion before we had crossed the dishevelled swaths.

Father asked: 'What about the Rackenfords?'

'We'll square the Rackenfords,' I said. 'They've only got to find a man. We have to find an heir.'

When we went back to the house for dinner I found that someone had left a letter from Mrs Mowbray on the table, telling me Dr Williams's address.

9

Now roses scramble over cottage doorways, smothering windows, spilling over garden hedges, while old men eke out their strength, leaning on their hoes above the huge shells and the stones, carefully whitewashed, that restrain sweet williams and pansies and wallflowers from overflowing crowded beds.

It is the time when midsummer flowers light the lanes for a short while before hedges and banks are cut back: musk mallow with pale rose-coloured flowers veined like a butterfly's wing and buds seamed together like needlework; toadflax, called 'butter and eggs', with yellow flowers spurred and splashed with orange; crowding purple and yellow vetches, and meadowsweet with honey-coloured, honey-scented flowers that have no honey. Drooping foxgloves, top-heavy with flowers, lean from the bracken-covered bank tops, and at their foot hedge bedstraw follows every curve with clustered flowers like a burden of bubbles.

They have such brief luxuriance. As soon as hay harvest is done the farmers will cut their banks and then the topic in the pub will be whether a stretch has been left undone because the owner cannot afford the wages for the labour.

Now the Sexton takes his hook to the ox-eye daisies that have whitened the churchyard for a month, and the mounds appear again, exposed and unfamiliar as a shorn flock of sheep. There is time, until corn harvest, to linger a little over jobs in the house, and in the evenings Peter and Simon come over to help to prolong them, hunting through the house, their voices drifting from room to room in the open summer atmosphere until they run me to earth.

'Good. She's ironing. Why d'you always iron in the bathroom, Luce?'

'Because I keep a spirit stove up here for the irons, and I can put the things straight into the airing cupboard when they're done.'

This question, with its answer, is traditional, and leads to the observation that ours is a pretty modern farmhouse; praise that I counter modestly with the assurance that someone has to pump the water by hand up to the cistern every day, and it ends with some boasting, by the boys, that one day they are going to have a motor to generate electricity to pump their water, light their house, and work a milking machine. It is a set-piece of conversation, like many others between neighbours who meet almost every day.

There is no need to ask where George is; he will be bedding the calves down, or judging an imaginary show; and no need to take my attention off my job while they stand about, noisily doing nothing, until they come to the point.

'Shall we play crosswords while you iron?' Neither is the spokesman. There is only a year between them, and they are like two dogs who answer to the name of either.

'Where are the papers and pencils, Luce?'

'In the cupboard, probably.'

I ask them, knowing that they will settle which one does it by some apparently silent communication, to make my paper ready, and to mark it darkly. One sits on the cork stool, the only seat in the room; without comment, the other puts down the cover on the only other resting-place and seats himself absent-mindedly, marking a paper with a square enclosing five spaces down and five across.

'Whose turn is it to start?'

'Simon's,' I say, without consideration, starting the dispute that will lead to a decision. The game calls for very little effort from me, for the real competition is between the boys, and while there is a great deal of arrangement, by them, so that neither shall see the other's game, it is understood that neither will look at mine, which lies at the end of the board so that I can fill it in while I iron.

We each choose a letter in turn, determined not to give away one the others will need, set on an unattained target of a finished square composed only of five-letter words downwards and across. Towards the end well-laid plans have to be abandoned, and the boys search for innovations with distracted looks which are never expended on life's problems, while I, less ambitiously, continue with my ironing.

'I say, how d'you spell chaos?'
'Chaos? that's a telephone box, isn't it?'
'Don't be a fool. That's a chaosk.'

At the end they exchange papers to add up the score, while I am trusted to declare my own.

'Here, what's this, Athen?'
'Never heard of Athen?'
'No. What is it?'
'A place.'

10

Dr Williams answered my letter with a printed book, and a letter which I read greedily before preparing breakfast.

'Of course I will take you as a pupil of my correspondence course, if you, on your part, would like it and could work in my way. I send you the Notes of the first part. Please read the preface and introduction, and if you approve of my method and are willing to follow the instructions, would you tell me so, and I will send you the two Braille books that go with these Notes.

'There is no charge. It is my one great pleasure, especially if my pupils learn to read successfully.' She went on to explain how she liked the work done, one lesson at a time, to be corrected with the Notes, and an exercise to be sent to her for correction; then, 'It is such a good thing that you can still write, and I think you will be able to see the Notes, because I have had them printed, for this very reason, in clear type with the letters and Braille signs in very clear print. . . . But of course, don't crib; that would spoil the fun. The great secret of learning is to keep your reading finger on the word you are reading and not to lift it off the page unless you carefully mark the place where you were, by counting the lines, or with a scrap of paper, or just with your other hand for a moment. And no looking at the Braille I give you to read, but train your fingers to do the work of your eyes. Be ingenious about it. It is a great joy to feel that you need not worry your poor eyes, I assure you.

'I have had much trouble, myself, and one day I shall not be able to read, but I have had several reprieves, for which I am thankful.'

While I read my letter the careful handwriting opened the room to a quiet invasion. In fields and lanes, in the village and farmhouses, our talk either leaves half the matter unsaid, for the hearer to fill in from imagination or experience, or repeats itself, with minute variations of detail, over and over again. We have no middle way between garrulity and reticence. Now a thoughtful presence, articulate in measured, simple words, took possession of the kitchen.

After breakfast I settled down to read the preface and introduction. I can hardly remember, now, what ideas I used to have about Braille. I suppose I understood, vaguely, that it is composed of a system of embossed dots. But now, discovering that the full Braille sign is like the six of dominoes placed on end, and that the other signs are composed of one or more of these dots, it seemed that I had always known it, and, as with so many discoveries, the satisfied mind said 'that is how it would be'. And always the teacher's personality shaped the instruction. 'Speed is greatly overrated in these hectic times, but it will come with patient concentration of purpose. You must coax your finger to make it out, and with a little initiative and humouring on your part it will respond. Don't fidget either your finger or yourself, but be quietly resolute.'

As I reached the first symbols of Braille the telephone clamoured, and I had to go out into the fields with an urgent plea from a neighbour for Father's help with haymaking.

To the sharpened perception of excitement it was very still in the middle of the twenty-acre field where Father stood among the last of his hay, which has been baled for storage in the tallets, and set up in pyramids of three, used for perches by solitary birds until it is carted. Sunshine filled the field and lit the tops of the heavy elms; and the enforced pause on the brink of discovery must have made me need to prolong the present moment, for now, instead of hurrying back to the house, I walked in a dream. The real world was unreal and yet as starkly clear as though a telescope picked out unheeded prospects and thrust them into sight.

On a bank between two pastures a tall bed of nettles leaned towards my path: dull-coloured flowers among leaves turning yellow, crowded with caterpillars, their velvet skins dark and covered with very small white spots, armed with spikes of steel blue that matched their armoured faces. Indifferent to the wind that heeled them back and forth in the sunshine, they moved hollowed rubber feet along the leaves, raising their polished masks blindly, stretching forward their shining faces, eating in a widening arc towards their bodies. Stupefied with content, full-fed they fell asleep coiled on the hairy surface of a leaf, rocked in the wind.

Sometimes in the past I have envied creatures whose world is a cabbage leaf or a hollow stump of wood. Now every reminder of cocooned oblivion is a dart aimed by fear and urgency. When I reached the house I wrote to Dr Williams asking for the two Braille books, and then I settled down to the first lesson.

For two days I have read, again and again, the introductory notes, and have learnt the symbols of the first seven selected letters; and all the time, as I have gone about my work, the substance of the book has been more solid than the farm, as though I saw all things from a distance. Yet, because almost everything I do I have done from childhood, my hands have carried on with their work.

The calves in their pens impatiently try to force my attention on them, loudly sucking the hem of my skirt with hard movements of their lips, nudging round foreheads greedily under the buckets I carry, butting and grunting with annoyance in a half-forgotten effort to hasten the flow of their mothers' milk. The one newly born, that is fed from a bucket of his own mother's milk, gets slowly to his feet, straightening his hind legs stiffly, rocking as he rests on his knees, gathering strength to straighten his forelegs. His mother would have nosed him, lowing throatily, until, after a fall or two, he would rest against her firm leg to raise his weight on his bent forelegs, straightening them tentatively until he stood on four hoofs, delicately cleft, of pure white horn. I put my hand over his nose, with the tips of my fingers between his tongue and the roof of his mouth, and he grips my fingers between tongue and palate and sucks while I draw his mouth to the surface of the milk, where he swallows noisily. From time to time he nudges his forehead upwards, angrily, or raises his mouth instinctively to search for his mother's teats, then he forgets the pail, and his nose has to be led back to it again. When the milk is finished he dances about, playing, until he frightens himself with his own excitement, and stops, prominent-eyed, head down and feet stubbornly planted, until at last he falls over and lies down sleepily on one flank, his forelegs tucked under him with rounded knees, his hindlegs drawn towards his belly. So he would have lain against his mother's protective side.

I have watched this sad, familiar little play in a dream into which, sometimes, the past has intruded unexpectedly.

Very young, calves grow sharp little spade-shaped teeth, which, if they close on the quick of your nails while the calf is sucking, cause a sickening twinge. Between breakfast and hurrying to the Vicarage lessons it used to be my job to feed the calves, and at the independent age of about eleven I came across a short length of narrow tubing somewhere, lying about, and with it the brilliant idea that, led from a bucket to a calf's mouth, it would spare me the sudden discomfort of nipping teeth. It also, as I discovered when I tried it, halved the time of feeding, for, pipe in mouth, each calf took in its allowance of milk in one almost breathless swallow. The experiment came to an end before Father unearthed it, for he observed, one day, 'Pot-bellied lot of calves us've got now,' and I knew that its day was done.

When I go into the fields I see the signs of the season, but am no longer part of it. I do not think it fanciful to believe that farm people are differently tempered during the different seasons; the urgency of tilling, the surge and luxuriance of haytime, the pregnant fulfilment of corn harvest, the sense of the year's running down in the shortening days of potato and root lifting, enlist us temperamentally. All our days pass linked on the chain of the farming seasons, remembered for their place in them. 'I zeed a covey o' partridges in the stream field last year,' Dick will say one day in winter. 'When was that?' 'When the corn were beginning to colour.'

Now I seem to see the summer maturing as one might look at a picture without its penetrating to the mind, knowing by heart how barley fields darken at this time of year, because, though the beard is still green, the upper surface of the ear grows rose-coloured; how the ears of oats silver as the sheaths of the grains whiten at the tips while the plants are still blue-green; how wheat is the yellowest green of all, the ears standing up sturdy and square.

In the summer wind a cornfield is never still. Oats, whitening in the sunshine, bleaching to the colour of pale tea, toss and bow with rising and falling of dry, brittle sighing that never dies; wheat, tanning in the sun, bends full ears stiffly with the stem, not drooping at the neck, like barley, which turns all its silken, bearded heads away from the wind. Butterflies, weaving in and out among the grasses of the headlands, fly in excited circles and settle, swaying, clinging to a grass stem with shadows of grasses flickering across their folded wings. I have seen it all as a background to the exploration I am about to make.

Two days after I opened the first of the books that Dr Williams sent me I received the two Braille books she had promised: the lesson book to study, and the exercises which I am to send to her. I had the instruction at heart, and the symbols of the seven letters of the first lesson—the easiest to feel—and five abbreviations. I brought a low table into the kitchen for the Braille book, and prepared to write out the lesson my finger read.

Peter and Simon wandered in. 'What about a game of something, Luce?'

'Games!' I said. 'I've no time for them. You can hear my lesson, if you like.'

I gave them the printed book, and they sat at the kitchen table, delighted, watchful as hunting cats, prepared to spring triumphantly on my mistakes.

I placed the forefinger of my left hand on the stiff brown page in front of me, and felt for the beginning of the first line. The country I had glimpsed when I held the cool poppy in my hand came into sight.

I am determined not to begin the exercise which I shall send to Dr Williams until I can read the first lesson perfectly. My mind's eye has the symbols, and while my finger is sensitive it cannot make a mistake, but feeling among the dots it quickly becomes dizzy. Yet already I have learnt one thing: the lighter the touch the easier it is to read. When sense will not come the temptation is to press harder, but only by feeling more lightly will reading go forward. My amateur finger so far can only retain its sensitivity for the length of five lines.

Since my initiation two days ago, with the boys, I have spent all my spare moments on the Braille pages of the lesson, and in the afternoon I have taken the printed book out of doors to read its introduction again.

I sit at the foot of the new rick, on some fallen hay, a resting-place, in sunshine, for butterflies flattening their wings and basking. At the bottom of the hedge, beside the rick, they probe pale thistle flowers, and rise, flying over my head, with a papery clatter of wings.

Insects fill the air, glimmering like motes in a shaft of sunshine, weaving, dipping, and rising again, and I can still see them while I listen to the curlews crying over the hayfield where cutting has disturbed their family. The young fly, crying anxiously all the while, with a whinnying shout, circling the higher field whither their parents call them, returning to their lost nesting place.

I have moved a step forward into my new country, for already reading with my hands increases the perception of senses other than sight. For a moment I live in two worlds, the country of the seeing and of the blind; and so I carry my notebook everywhere, to try to catch, in the open air, the essence of things seen, perhaps for the last time, and truly heard for the first.

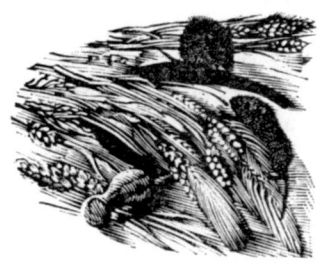

12

On the way to the village I stopped to call on Nancy's mother. Sunlight slanted between the leaves of clustered pots of geraniums on the kitchen window-sill, paling the green, tasselled valance on the dark chimneypiece, and the faded woollen tablecloth; finding, before it was lost among the furniture, ornaments, photographs and keepsakes crowding the little room, the quiet face of Mrs Eastcott with the erased expression of one for whom memory is more potent than the living scene. (Was it, I wondered, like the face of someone—blind?)

The hot, sleepy smell of the sunned geraniums filled the room with the climate of afternoon; the greenish light from the window lent it the colour of an overcrowded aquarium. A raised voice reminded us of neighbours on the other side of the wall.

I said: 'I hear they are making trouble for Nancy again.'

'Strife-makers,' replied Mrs Eastcott, without heat.

Comely in youth, with the dark beauty Nancy has inherited, defiant in middle age, she has grown placid now, and fatalistic, translating the incidents of her life into the terms of folk tales linked by the coincidences and chance meetings natural in a community all known to one another personally or by hearsay. 'What is to be will be.' Her creed touches Nancy's predicament in the threat of insanity fostered by the neighbours.

It is wonderful that Nancy has the patience to return all

the accumulated mementos of the past to their places when she turns out the room for her mother. It is even more remarkable that this room—where it is hardly possible to look out of the window—and one of the two bedrooms above it, enclosed Harry Eastcott's home life. It occurs to me now that it may have been one of the reasons for his behaviour during his last year, when overtaken by nightfall and sleep as he vaguely pottered about on his piece of land he would lie down in one of his sheds, and taking a liking to the life would sleep out for several nights on end.

Land workers, notoriously, like to shut themselves in when they shake off the elements on their doorstep, but Harry was a man with one ear always cocked towards the world outside. All the other land workers I have known were employed on farms, but Harry never worked regularly for a master. Besides his own half acre of garden he tilled a few acres rented from my father, and supported his family on the profits from pigs, fowls, vegetables, rabbit catching and higgling; and in the time generously snatched from these labours he looked round. Most farm workers have a store of natural information. Life-learnt weather lore and the prophecies that depend on the movements of birds and insects, animals, frogs and toads, are part of their equipment. But Harry's mind was furnished with accumulated observations unconnected with the pursuit of his livelihood: deductions made for their own sake, pondered on only for their interest; and by the time of my childhood his collection had expanded into an untabulated museum of facts round which he was ready to conduct another collector, comparing, advising, exchanging.

'Have you ever noticed, Harry, how sharp the country looks in a north wind?' (Have you ever noticed! You, who never ceased to notice such things.)

With a connoisseur's attention he would study my find, and match it with one of his own. 'It dries up the crests o' the ploughland, don't it, so that the furrows are all dark, bent to the shape o' the fields.'

Then he would consider his own miscellany. 'Now, when you get a westerly gale the fields in the distance are covered wi' a veil of misting wet. And a south-west wind, that darkens everything, makes it rich and damp. But an east wind lightens it, washes it out, like. Have you ever seen how the sunshine in an east wind finds out the grey in the hedges? An east wind ages the land, dries out the pastures and ploughland till they'm all pale and old looking.'

In those days I had little in my collection to show him, almost nothing to exchange. But any discovery of mine, brought out for inspection, set him rummaging in his store to enrich mine.

'Have you ever seen, Harry, how after a season when there have been hundreds of butterflies—Painted Ladies, say— sometimes there'll be almost none next year?'

'Reckon 'tis over-crowding does it,' he said, 'like with any other livestock. Soon as there's too many they get diseased, or some enemy gets at em, then, next season, they'm scarce.'

One evening, when I climbed through the gap in the hedge on to his piece of land, I found him bending over a flat wooden box. It was only a week or two since he had come out of hospital after the accident that embittered the end of his life. His vegetable garden was overgrown and unkempt, the muck from the pigsties still waiting to be carried away from the untidy heaps where Mrs Eastcott had dumped it while she struggled on in his absence. Certainly he did not look fit for work. But he bent over a wooden box covered by a sheet of glass weighted by a few small pebbles.

'What have you got?' I asked.

He raised his head. He was the most striking looking man I have ever seen, all the lines of his face convex, save for the deep, straight furrows reaching from below each cheek-bone to the corners of his mouth. He had the curving profile of a Roman, his nose reproducing the forehead's arc, where deep lines curved roundly above arched and jutting eyebrows. When I remember him—whenever something, unnoticed before, reveals itself out of doors—I wonder from what crevice in time that face was washed back into circulation.

His eyes met mine evasively. He was taken by surprise.

'A slug,' he said defensively.

While I made some astonished reply he regained his composure, and asked whether I had noticed that the great brown slugs that left a trail of slime and destruction on our seed beds every night could stretch to a length of about two and a half inches, or draw themselves up into a hard ball.

'Times,' he said, 'I've wanted to know how much they could lift when they hump up like that.' So he had put one in a box with a piece of glass on top, weighted with stones. 'In the cool o' the evening I hope this un'll hump up between the glass and the box and get out. Does, I'll put another un in wi' more stones on un tomorrow.'

I believe it was later in the same summer when he called me through the gap in the hedge to look at the caterpillars, climbing up the side of the dilapidated wooden shack where he kept his tools, to become chrysalises under the shelter of the eaves. For days, he said, they have been leaving his cabbages, creeping across the rough earth and up the wall, where, reaching the top, they dawdled about, often for a day, until they began to spin the girdle that would bind them to the wall.

For a moment we watched one which ejected the silken thread from its mouth, bending its head back over its body, swaying from side to side, mouth working, diligently fixing the cord to the wall on either side of it, and another which stretched and heaved until the finished girdle was about a third of the way down its back.

'Like a lady getting into her stays,' Harry observed appreciatively. 'When they finish they look as if they'm praying,' he added, and showed me one already in the long sleep of transformation, wings and antennae pressed on its back under the hardening shell, the upper part of its body drawn away from the wall beneath the bowed head, and below it the old shrivelled skin armed with its black mask. But that was not what he had called me to see. There was one, perfectly still and in the position the others had taken, but without the girdle. While we watched, a writhing mass erupted from each side of the creature: maggots were emerging, stretching and wriggling, 'Like little pigs suckling at a sow, only they'm both sides.' Harry broke the sickening silence.

'They'm grubs o' the fly as'll lay its eggs under the skin o' caterpillars, next year, and kill em.'

In a very short time the grubs developed a woolly haze and soon formed a compact mass of cocoons covered with sulphur-coloured wool, with the caterpillar, moribund, arched over them.

'Er'll die in that position, and stay to protect her murderers till her dried body drops off,' Harry said. 'There were a gurt lot o' butterflies this year, because, I reckon, these enemies of theirn were scarce. But there won't be so many next year, or the year after.' Then he added a typical conclusion: 'Nature's never in debt for long.'

After his accident people noticed how he began to talk, not only to himself, but to animals, birds, and even trees. They shook their heads and pursed their lips and speculated, though without risking the violent reply they guessed would be returned, had they asked questions, when they saw him on successive days of summer under trees whose branches he was beating with a pole above an open umbrella, inverted and with its ferrule firmly planted in the ground. His unusualness was hardening into oddity; but if anyone had dared to enquire they would have found that some of his freaks, at least, were not motiveless. For in the case of the tree-beating he had told me, long before, that he had thought of a way of bringing down some kind of rare caterpillar with an open umbrella and a pole.

People said that he would call birds to perch on his head and shoulders during the days that he spent aimlessly, by local standards, on his plot of land, and they excused his gainless ways of filling in his time by saying that he had gone queer. It was not until he began sleeping rough that a core of severe disapproval revealed itself, and a note of harshness crept into their murmuring, as though they were afraid the habit were catching, and they began to make it clear that the Eastcotts were a drag on the village's good name.

But still, when Harry was able to work, and did not decide

to leave the management of his holding to Nature to pay her debts in her own time, the smallest stroke of good fortune was enjoyed by his family almost within minutes of its arrival. If he made a good bargain with his stock of various kinds, a celebration began at once. It is a way of life which, for all its miseries, has a lively savour untasted by the cautious; but even this was snatched away by a typical stroke of bad management. One night, when Nancy was about fifteen, a truck drove into Harry's unlighted cart while he was coming home from a sale, and he and the horse were killed.

Nancy, isolated by the family pride, grew up without the consolation of her father's disdain for appearances. Her two brothers, younger than she, fared better. After the manner of younger members of families whose circumstances have worsened, they grew up seasoned to the new climate, stolidly ignoring any half-pitying, half-critical undertones that reached them, until, finishing their brief schooling, they found jobs on farms; but then, as if by natural inclination, the work they engaged on took them, gradually, a little farther from the neighbourhood.

Yet Nancy has an endowment from her father: the gift of unstudied affinity with her surroundings, as though Harry's lifelong observation, grafted on to her mother's legacy of feeling, flowered in understanding. As well as foretelling the storm, and the coming thaw in the throes of hard weather, she anticipates the awkward behaviour of difficult animals, and by forestalling it has earned herself a reputation for clever handling, though the village congratulates itself, also, on noticing that even this gift is 'a bit queer'.

 # 13

At half-past six in the morning, which is really half-past five, mist encircles the house; even the nearest pasture oak is beyond the horizon within whose small circle the grass is very green, soaking with dew; and the geese, sitting leisurely, groom themselves carefully, loose feathers falling lightly on the grass as they comb their breasts with deep, downward strokes of their beaks.

Presently the cows break slowly through the horizon, heads low, planting each foot deliberately on the muddy track into the yard, changing their weight very slowly from foot to foot as they feel the rough, stony surface under the mud which daily treading has worked to the consistency of thick, deep cream. As each cow reaches the hard surface of the yard she stands, or moves even more slowly than before, jostling her gathering fellows, lunging a heavy head sideways to rasp her flank with her tongue, swinging her tail indolently in a half circle until the switch lies on her back then falls to rise in a matching arc on the other side. All prolong the moment until they will lift their feet again, and, with a heavy outward breath, take the low step into the shippon where they are milked. By the time they are in, the pasture trees are a form in the mist, a deeper dove-colour than the surrounding atmosphere which thins, during milking, until the trees stand clear, with their shadows beneath them on the grass where the dew still lies like frost. There is not yet sunshine, only lightness.

While I feed the calves the sun overtops the house, lighting the hay in the tallet and the tunnels the cats have made between the bales leading to their sleeping places, where hens astonish them by laying in the daytime.

Father came to the door of the shippon. 'An old friend of ours has come back,' he said; and when I had fed the calves I hurried across the yard to greet Willmouse, who returned me the dogged, cynical stare of a tramp.

In the kitchen the house cats crouched on the dresser waiting to drop, like sea birds, on the pan of milk they were expecting me to put on the floor. Only Aubrey, the half-grown tabby who has come, seemingly full Persian, from a smooth, etch-striped mother, slept, indifferent, on the worn velvet cushion of an armchair, curled with his head on the tip of his tail, with no contours, his tiger markings merging in the thick, soft fur like the colours of a moth. If he should move he would condescend to share the cushion only with a favoured half-brother, or with his mother, whose latest family is still unweaned. Purring loudly, he steals her milk, pressing her belly with strong paws, while her breasts, delicate pink, rise through the creamy fur, faintly flushed domes which Aubrey robs luxuriously.

Now the mother cat was sitting on the dresser at an autocratically measured distance from three others of her offspring: Aubrey's sister, black and fluffy, the other two matching the mother's stencilled coat of black and silver, in which each hair is flecked with light and dark, like the fur of a wild rabbit. Homely and ingratiating in the daytime, they are all only partly domesticated, using the comforts of the house, maintaining their right to the jungle life outside. The young cats are allowed indoors only by their mother's permission, which she revokes without warning; they have each forced their way in by persistence and strength of character, and live within a hair's breadth of expulsion.

In winter, when the cats sit by the hearth, murmuring and growling, their ears bent towards the purring fire, the mother, smooth as polished wood, always in the middle, only Aubrey attempts to creep up beside her. As he moves, his deep fur ripples, the stripes of his tabby coat breaking and rejoining with the moving texture of watered silk. The mother cat does not notice him until she must, then, lashing out with arched claws, she buries her talons in the soft, effeminate fur, and he, crouching frozen, shrinks away when he dares to move.

Two kittens danced in the yard outside, black, stiff-legged, with tails like pencils, moving suddenly in unexpected side-leaps, shaking a front or hind paw with pantomime fastidiousness if they touched the stream of water running away from the dairy, placing their feet with exaggerated precision between the puddles. They made advances to Willmouse, whose muttered threat dispersed them like scattered leaves.

I put down a pan of milk and called Willmouse in. He shouldered the door open and scowled maliciously round the corner. The cats fled back to the dresser and sat looking down on him while he finished their milk: the mother cat; Fanny and Sophie, her daughters of different generations; and Fred, Aubrey's hanger-on.

Fred's gaze was candidly admiring. When he was young he mortgaged his whole future in one act of spectacular daring, leaping, with a mouse he had caught, from an upstairs window into the yard. The shock of his landing must have injured him in some way, for he grew no more, but dwindled, rather, into a wizened, apologetic little dwarf whom Aubrey, surprisingly, took under his protection, granting him, in return for constant attendance and unresisting acceptance of capricious bullying, the patronage of an overlord. Fred looked down at Willmouse, the only full-grown tom he had ever seen, and the expression in his protruding eyes seemed to disclose certain comparisons passing through his foggy mind.

Fanny, pretty, silly little Fanny, yawned, throwing back her fluffy dark feather-pate to exhibit her pink tongue and all her pointed teeth in a flashing smile. It is wonderful that such an addle-head ever won admittance to the house. She has shown such persistence only once again, when, losing her own kittens from neglect—she and Fred slept on them one sunny afternoon in the yard on a wisp of hay—she stole Sophie from the mother cat's nest in the tallet and kept her, secretly, in a loft above the barn, and waited again, with the timeless patience of animals, until the mother cat—who had at once found her kitten and returned it to her own nest—went hunting next day; then the little black cat carried it down the tallet steps, across the yard, up the steps into the loft, her head held high and forelegs stiff and straight, repeating her theft until the doubly fed kitten grew too heavy for either cat to carry, and they compromised, alternately removing it to nests they each made in the loft.

Fanny prolonged her smile, and yawned again to renew it.

Plump young Sophie looked down with bored distaste on the old man splashing messily beneath her. The mother cat, lean and sleek and relaxed, disguising the reserved tautness of a new spring, sat with her cool ears pointed towards the visitor, ears with fur short and smooth as lichen on a stone, and showed no interest at all.

Yet once Willmouse was his mother's favourite kitten, the first solitary kitten she ever had; for during the first few years of her maturity, punctuated by noisy honeymoons with a taciturn visiting tom, she repopulated the yard when the community had been wiped out by cat 'flu, and earned herself her title, distinct from the chance names bestowed, on an impulse, on her descendants. By the time Willmouse was born her work was done. We had enough cats to keep down vermin in storehouses and rickyards and barns, and returned to our careful practice of allowing the mothers to keep only one or two of each litter.

The mother did her kitten so well, in his nest in the tallet, that soon after his eyes opened she was unable to pick him up by the scruff of his fat little neck, and she was forced to carry him by one ear. The dark marking on her coat was reproduced on his as jersey-stripes fitting so tightly round his well-fed little body that he seemed always on the point of bursting out of his clothes, and when she bumped him down the steps from the tallet, held by one ear, he looked as though he must fall through his skin; until, one sunny morning, she was left on the steps with the top of his ear still between her teeth, and her son lay kicking at the bottom. It was only by that sawn-off ear that I recognized the broad-cheeked bull-necked villain outside, this morning.

Poor little Willmouse. His nursery days over, his mother decided to make him brave. She, herself, had had a strange upbringing. Deserted by her mother when she was a fortnight old, she was reared by our old sheepdog bitch, who, in excess of love, came into milk, and nursed her with the bewildered maternity of a hen with a brood of ducklings; though when the kitten grew to maturity neither of them showed any recognition of their former relationship. The cat remembered only, with supercilious familiarity, that her poor old foster-mother hated to have her forepaws touched, and as they sat before the fire, the cat, who would always be exactly in the middle, would pat the dog's toes so that she retreated inch by inch, leaving her tormentor in the best position. The mother cat taught this trick to every kitten she allowed into the house, so that on a winter day, until the dog died of old age, a row of cats basked before the fire between her and the blaze.

Whatever shortcomings there may have been in her own bringing-up the mother cat made good in the raising of Willmouse. With a purring, deep-throated, maternal call that contained, very soon, a note of anxiety, she summoned him to cut off her sallies when they played round the chair legs in the kitchen, until he learnt cautiously to stay behind, for when she caught him she held him down with her teeth and forepaws, savagely battering him with strong hind feet. If he tumbled after her tail she turned and taught him to fight, and when she called to him from the top of the tallet steps he soon learnt to stay where he was, for if he reached the top the chance was strong that she would push him off to make him brave. Mouse after mouse she brought in for him wearily to repeat the actions of tracking and murder; and when she was satisfied with his proficiency, but far, far too soon for Willmouse, she presented him with young rats, carefully preserved alive.

Toms are the most lovable kittens, but almost all the farm cats are queens, for as soon as the males reach maturity they wander, returning only at rare intervals, losing all homeliness. But Willmouse stayed with us for two years. His lessons in bravery had reduced him to a grovelling little coward, careful of sudden noises, wary of shadows, but confiding and charming to Father and me. Then, one day, we found he had left us. He had grown up overnight.

After breakfast I fetched paraffin and cleaned Willmouse up. His ear and a half, I had discovered at our meeting, were outlined with rabbit fleas. He showed no appreciation, but I am glad that I did it, for by evening, after thoroughly upsetting everybody, he had gone. Perhaps his return was as much a failure for him as for me. He seemed not to have foreseen any changes during his absence, and the presence of the kittens in the yard blighted his homecoming even before we met. A vengeful Peter Pan, he stalked through the buildings, threatening and glowering, until the cat population, cornered in their secret hiding places, vanished for the day.

After tea there were muffled cries from the chair in the kitchen. Fred, who can never know whether he is invited on to Aubrey's cushion to be used for a pillow, to play, to wash his master, or be beaten, was feebly resisting a hiding of unprecedented vigour. During the afternoon Aubrey, peacocking across the yard, had passed Willmouse, who dismissed him with a scowl; but Aubrey had reached the spot where he invariably pauses to look back to see that his perfect tail is clear of the ground. It was unlucky for Fred, pressing, as always, close to his master, that he should have been caught by his patron at that moment with his pop-eyes resting with unreserved admiration on the piratical features and burly frame of Willmouse the Brave.

I parted them before I brought out the Braille exercise book and, with paper and pencil, set to work on the first exercise to be sent to Dr Williams for correction. I have spent a week going over the first lesson again and again, and as my finger moused along the untried dots I found, this time, that it spelt out the small phrases at once; the simple phrases of a child's first reading book, which I leapt on with triumph and wrote down with my right hand while the left spelt out the words:

                I am Mab
                I am like Mab
                I am almost like Mab etc.,

until all the letters and all the abbreviations of the first lesson had been used several times. After ten minutes I allowed my tipsy finger a rest, and then continued for a quarter of an hour until the harvest of my first week's work was gathered on the paper beside me.

                I am for Mamma but I am for Mab also
                I am also for more lamb for us. . . .

I was sorry that the boys were not with me. Yet they might have been shocked at my ingenuous delight.

With eyes closed I can hear that corn harvest is near and haytime over. The wind is heavy in the trees, bowing the oats with the rustle of paper as they toss and bend and circle distractedly, and hiss and rave; great waves run over the barley field, and small whirlpools eddy and cease. The goslings have forgotten how to whistle, and utter croaks of varying, unexpected pitch. Curlews no longer call; young buzzards slip from dense trees, mewing nervously; and from a pile of sere hedge-cuttings comes the bell-call of a grown family of blue tits as they play among the brittle twigs. Small flocks of chaffinches rise from the lane and scold from the hedges. It is a restless time, the slack tide of summer before the onrush of harvest sweeps the farming community into urgent activity, or the briskness of autumn dictates a pattern of winter behaviour to the year's young wild life in fields and hedges.

Father came in for breakfast wearily, stooping, older than his age. I told him, as often before, that he should see a doctor, and he replied, as I guessed he would: 'At my age a man's a fool or his own physician.'

Before I had time to suggest, as he knew I would, that he should take a rest before harvest, he countered, in the level voice that lets fall a surprise—his voice, I believe, would make no distinction between announcing our bankruptcy or the winning of a football pool—'Us'll spend today on the Moor.'

Everyone has his own spring of well-being. I believe neither of us ever walks out under the open sky without a lift of the heart; but our own fields impinge on our attention like clamouring children, and when we need a rest we leave them.

Unless it is briefly hidden by the weather Dartmoor is always in sight of the farm, reflecting the mood of the sky: pale in wind and showers, yet sharply outlined; almost lost on still, moist days, having only a shade more substance than the clouds; blue in days of high summer; bland and green in spring; brown in winter, the thoroughfare of huge cloud shadows. We may not purposely keep it in mind, but it is hardly ever forgotten for long, if only because it foreshadows the weather, and it is in keeping with its nature that its portents are usually for the worse. Placid sunshine on our fields may smooth the wilderness into a disguise of domesticity; but when its lesser hills stand sharp against its rock-strewn heights the fairest prospects on our level are a lie. Winter's first snow lies on its crests. It is hard weather's accomplice.

Few of its farmers can never have lost a beast in snowdrift or bog or flood, or themselves have not faced disaster while rescuing their stock, and they are not the ones to under-estimate its possibilities or belittle experience for want of eloquence. Our folklore and fireside tales of haunted bogs and travellers wandering, pixy-led, have evolved in its obliterating mists and the soft, insistent rain (so habitual that it is scarcely perceived until it ceases) which feeds its morasses. Its legendary black dogs and ghostly riders and spectral packs of hounds are revived by the lightning of its violent storms playing among the littered rocks of its solitary wastes and the stone circles and memorials of its ancient dead.

It is never mere scenery to us, and now when I try to visualize it I cannot define its magnitude. Only incidents in its existence come into mind: how the foam beneath a fall of rock, where brown water buries itself in the pool below, is the green-white of flowers, rising in a leaping tongue to disturb smooth water where some bubbles escape destruction and sail in a twisting, eddying line over the sepia stones of the stream's bed to the next fall; bursting, joining and parting, while the stream triumphantly drowns every other sound, with slide and rush and hiss and the deep rumble of its fall over the rocks at the pool's edge, like voices joined in endless argument.

What is the colour of the Moor? Often I have tried to discover. Seen from its own slopes, except during late summer's triumph of gorse and heather, it is roughly the colour of mown hay, traversed by paths, the width of a boot, of dried, worn grass and cracked peat, winding round heather plants and boulders, avoiding wet beds of moss, followed by sheep who move head down, nose following tail, unhurried, relentless as water.

But today no sheep were to be seen on the steep valleys' sides. The village where we left the car, usually silent in mid-morning, was full of the sound of bleating flocks impounded in stone-walled fields. It was the day of compulsory sheep dipping. Only a crowd of ponies, bleached and rain-washed as their background, disturbed by the sheep drive, stood above the road with manes and tails flaring in the wind.

Down by the noisy river a flock moved towards the village, the deep cry of ewes and high bleating of lambs and the repeated barking of a dog rising to drown the voice of the river. While they streamed past us the dog leapt on to a boulder to watch them flow under him, treading a familiar path through the bracken, ewes calling to lambs who answered dams they could not recognize by their scent since they had been dipped. When they had passed, the sound of the river rose again, but only momentarily, for cries of sheep came faintly from the village, drawing nearer, and the high, insistent barking of a dog, and another flock moved into the pound trodden already with multitudes of slotted footprints, where two men refilled the pool with buckets of water from the river, dying it saffron-coloured, the ticklish smell of Derris overcoming, for once, the sheep-smell that usually lingers there.

Grey fleeces filled the space between four grey walls, black faces framed with curving horns crested the waves of grey:

surging, jostling, bleating, until they were lifted into the water and dipped with an inverted crutch, dipped as they swam, with meditated gentleness, rising and sinking, climbing the shallow steps at the farther end, standing to shake their fleeces, pale honey-coloured from the dye; then, for the first time since they were put into the water, they bleated.

A rainstorm obliterated all but the pound, while we watched: slanting rain, grey as the sheep, the boulders, and the sky, melting us into a scarcely visible feature of the hillside with the mosses of saffron and lemon and coral and black, and the diminutive flowers scattered in the wiry turf; dissolving us, with sundew and bog asphodel, heather and whortleberry and overcrowding bracken, into the ochre and orange, lilac and carmine and gaudy green, that compose the quiet-coloured mass, the sky's enigmatic companion, which has filled half our horizon all our lives when we lift our eyes from the fields.

15

The cows lie under the pasture trees while I walk across under their indolent gaze to fetch them in for milking, shouting to them to get up, aware of the eyes bent on me in languid speculation, and realizing, suddenly, that they know by heart the sequence of my movements as exactly as I know theirs: how they lie on one flank, chewing, their lower jaws moving elliptically to the slow rhythm of the strong muscles of their cheeks, their forelegs bent under them, their udders, large and full, resting on one leg, the other lazily stretched, while they turn their heads idly towards me, switching the end of their tails. Always they wait until I have reached the one farthest away before rising very slowly to their feet, heaving themselves ungraciously to their knees, straightening their hindlegs until their rumps are in the air swaying ponderously, stretching one foreleg and then the other, until at last they move forward unwillingly, pausing to relieve themselves with hindlegs spread wide and tails grotesquely twisted in the air. At the gateway into the yard they stand while an immutable order of precedence is observed, Rose, the 'master' cow, passing through first, the rest following in a sequence which no urging from the driver and no threats will alter.

But today Rose was in the farthest corner of the field where, with the inspired perversity of animals for choosing the least convenient place or wished-for moment, she had given birth to a calf. She bent her huge head over her son; she must have nosed him to his feet some time before, for he stood fairly steadily, stiff-legged, with his tail tucked in and head low, while he searched for her udder, nuzzling the skin of her flank with the tip of his tongue, making tentative sucking movements with his lips.

Rose finished licking her child, licking and lowing continuously with the short, softened voice of maternity, and pulled grass hungrily, continuing her lowing while she grazed, bending her neck to look at her son who staggered towards her dripping teats but could not find them. She moved a hindleg backwards to expose her udder, and continued grazing. I left them while I fetched the rest of the cows in, the next after Rose in order of supremacy taking the lead.

After milking we brought the calf in, riding in the link-box behind the tractor with its head in my lap as it lay in the hay. The mother followed, anxiously lowing, stroking it with her tongue, nervously trusting. We put it in a pen, deep in straw. The mother, from habit, walked into the shippon. They will not see one another again.

All night Rose cried for her calf, standing in the pasture at the yard gate, and all the next day. In the evening she stood alone by the gate as the herd moved slowly down the field on their way to a distant pasture where they like to sleep. When they were out of hearing she turned and went heavily after them, the habit of going with the herd at last overcoming maternal instinct.

16

When everyone else is busy with their corn harvest Mr Luppett saves his hay. He tills no corn on his north-facing land, and he is in no hurry to mow the hay that ripens later than his neighbours' on the other side of the valley.

When our barley stands with drooped head and the harvest begins, Mr Luppett brings out his old horse rake; and the light, grasshopper-ticking of its bouncing wheels joins with the heavier clacking of the reaper-and-binder's windmill arms on our side of the valley, and the slow, heavy drumming of a combine harvester reaping and thrashing as it crawls over the fields of a distant farm.

While Mr Luppett's fields lie quiet-coloured, lined with swaths of curing hay, ours are patterned with sheaves of corn resting head to head, peaked and crested, stooked on shining stubble; and all the sounds of harvesting bring back to sight the bearded ears of barley splaying outwards from the binding twine; and how oats curve, sheaf above sheaf, the drooping grains like painted tears; and how wheat sheaves stand firm and robust.

Excited cries announce the arrival of the boys who always come just as the last square of the field is cut—some magic telling them when it has been reached—to creep between the standing corn and drive the rabbits, which have retreated inwards all day, towards the men with guns. Hoarse whispers give away the intention of more agile ones, who fall on their crouching quarry with amazing dexterity, despatching them with a blow on the back of the head, throwing them on to the growing heap of mouse-coloured bodies with the wheaten fur on their flanks distinctive of harvest rabbits, which will be divided between the workers at the end of the day.

Everywhere the colour of cornfields surrounds us, and I remember how, as a child, I thought that stooked fields on distant hills looked like crimped heads of tight curls of close-cut hair, and beans, blackened by the sun, the leaves charred and twisted, like dark tents, when they were stooked on their black stubble with the bare red earth between.

In the opulent sunshine of midday the birds cease from calling, beasts crowd under hedges, and the geese, who graze in the pasture and sip dew off the grass in the cool of the morning, flop in a patch of shade and sleep, head under wing.

Between one and two all sound of harvesting dies; deep shadow fills the implement shed; a hen pecks steadily in an overturned bucket with a noise like dripping water. At the sound of a footfall in the yard one of the pigs will bark, and disturbing the others, lumber up from its sleep on the cool floor of the sty where they lie cheek to cheek. After they have all yelped expectantly they fall to bickering, irritable in the heat, until, after some grunting and squealing, they settle down again on their rustling bed and snore.

The cows come back to the yard half way through the afternoon, troubled by flies, and quarrel round the trough, horning one another out of the way, putting their tongues in to taste, drinking deep with their lips beneath the surface of the water, blowing out their cheeks, sucking noisily, lifting their heads to stare round with water running out of their mouths, lavish and extravagant; until, at half-past four, pails rattle in the dairy, the shippon door, which scrapes the ground, is dragged open, and they are driven in, slow footed, making a dry sound on the concreted yard. One will moo, another knocks over a pail, there is a sound of disturbed footfalls as one tries to horn another, then the rattle of chains as Dick fixes them in their standings. The calves, anxious for their feed, look over the hedge and bleat fretfully. A curtain stirs by an open window; the house is filled with the dry smell of warm timber: the languorous smell of indoor summer afternoon.

The village repeats the torpor of the yard, deserted even by the old men who potter in and out of the shops and spin out a pint at the Tenor Bell, who are out in the harvest fields now, giving help that is very welcome and advice that is not. So, when I called at the Bell to ask the landlord whether he could bring over some cider for the reapers, because I can no longer drive the car to fetch it, I was surprised to hear sounds, animated though subdued, of conversation within the open doorway. Leaning on the bar was a row of men, their identity confirmed by the presence of our undertaker, Jim's uncle, whom they had evidently fetched out for a drink; and I knew, then, that if I could have seen them clearly they would have been unmistakable in their black clothes. They were indulging in bland, discreet reminiscence, shoulder to black shoulder with their pints before them.

'Tell ee a thing I was said to the other day. . . .' Then followed a few quick words and a pause filled with muffled laughter. When I left, I passed what I had not discerned before: a hearse drawn up beside the pavement at a tactful distance up the road.

On the bridge I stopped to listen to the voices of the river, deep toned where it falls over granite blocks between grey buttresses, high and talkative as it continues over shallow stones and the weeds contending in its grasp. Cattle grazed beyond the bushes, the noise of their crisp pulling, swallowing and deep outward breaths almost stifled by the river's sound. A pair of moorhens crossed noisily, jerking heads red-fronted, each dividing the water in an arrowhead, dimly seen, half remembered. Presently one reappeared from under the bushes beside the arch within my small field of sight. She walked at the water's edge, lifting each foot out of the water, delicately stepping, jerking her head as she had when swimming, while she fished, searching the shallows, dipping her head to pick up what she had found. Then she moved under the bridge and was lost from sight.

It was as though a piece of music had stopped. I cannot remember exactly how she looked. Did the white feathers on each side of her tail flash as she walked? I do not know. I remember only how delicately she picked up each green foot and stepped forward in the bright water.

17

At the edge of the cornfields the pods of vetch in the hedge banks burst open in the sunshine with a sharp crack while the small flat pods of tares sprawling among the grasses explode with a smaller, duller sound. I have to walk round the harvest fields now, rather than across the stubble, because the rough ground which has had no direct contact with rain for months, and the spiked lines of cut stems, are too uneven for my misty sight. Every season will put its own minor hazards in my way, but I am used to the obstacles on familiar paths.

They are building the first of the ricks: Jim, Archie Wrangways, Dick and my father; Dick kneeling on the growing beehive shape placing the sheaves while the others pitch from the loaded trailer. Whoever looks up sees Dick's gnome-face looking down, and he has breath, while no one else has, for reminiscence when they knock off for a pull of sweet tea or cider. 'There were a pub I used to go to, when I were a young man, that drew cider in mugs wi' a lady on em. All in fancy clo'es she were, the way they handed the mug to ee. But when you turned un round she were naked. Yes, naked she were.' Then he begins the story again.

Archie listens with the sceptical bearing of one old man listening to another showing off. Jim does not say much, but I know how a flicker of appreciation will animate his placid face. Stocky and capable, he does not show that he notices how the two old men manoeuvre to leave the hardest work to him—pitching sheaves from the sloping field on to the trailer they are almost sure to find themselves on the upper side where the height is less—but in the evening he takes home a tale of the day's amusements to Nancy and her mother, which Nancy tells me while we work in the house. By then they are stories which have gained by the experience of all three, and by observation in which shrewdness is undistracted by sophistication or overmuch reading.

As the sun sinks, the baby buzzards begin to mew, sitting on the branches of the hedge oaks, afraid to make the flight across the field's width. While we walk back to the house they cease from crying; roosting birds twitter and rustle on their perches; the calves pull grass in their field for the last feed of the day; a cricket shrills in the garden; a cow coughs noisily in a distant pasture; a little owl calls cuck-cuck-cu-cu-cuck; a solitary engine goes along the line.

On such an evening small clouds that have been swept into shapes of plumes of feathers lie still, fading on the western sky; wisps and veils of cloud, coloured like the lining of a seashell, lie over the dark line of the Moor and the level chain of smoke that the train left behind; suddenly a star shines above them.

This morning Dr Williams returned my first Braille exercise, saying 'Well done. Now I know that you will learn all right and enjoy it. . . . I should like you to keep on with your writing: it is something you must keep up, always, even if the worst should come. It gives one a feeling of independence which is most valuable at all times of stress and difficulty.' And I have gone about my work hugging my small achievement, storing the present for the future; confident, now, that I shall learn to read with my finger and see by memory.

'Papa's bull is for sale for a small sum.' Reading a Braille exercise to the boys, the disastrous import of this sentence brought work to a standstill while they discussed a catastrophe so near to their hearts. When she returned the last exercise Dr Williams wrote that it had needed a good deal of patience and ingenuity to concoct 'some sort of sensible stuff' with the few fairly simple words at her disposal, and said she hoped her pupils could sometimes laugh at her sentences.

Little Mab's appearances under my tentative finger provoke a storm of derision from the audience, which the news that she likes kisses but is more for ices has not allayed. During the last lesson Dr Williams's ingenuity revealed itself in her most fantastic and delightful invention so far: 'Almost all people can poke up a calm mule.'

We finished the exercise: 'Sales for small sums seem a loss,' heartily corroborated by the boys, who read me the lessons in the printed book and Dr Williams's comments on my work.

I can no longer read by sight, and see all things, now, more in imagination than reality, hardly believing that I do not see; exploring the world of intuition and sound all the time. Every tree has a voice in the wind: the continuous murmur of an elm is only a sigh in an oak: a gentle rise and fall of branches. An ash keeps up a constant whisper as the narrow leaves move.

There is some indefinable hint of autumn in the air. The sunshine is mature and hot, yet its very affluence brings the memory of sudden frosts. Neighbours' voices carry across the fields, not with the sudden sweet clearness of haytime, when a wandering evening wind carries from distant fields voices that are lost as it dies, but full and resonant, as though the sky had come down and the air were denser to penetrate. Swifts, which yesterday circled anxiously and low, today are gone. From every stubble field pigeons get up with a wooden clap of wings.

In my vegetable garden insects hum in the rich, humid air; the heavy sunshine is almost a weight. A tall line of runner beans stoops under a burden of foliage and long rasping pods. Scarlet flowers, dimly seen, which will never fruit, still light the top; beneath them winter greens grow in profusion of huge, moisture-cupping leaves. The earth is damp and red and strong-smelling and I know how dew fills the cups where the leaves of brussels sprouts plants join the stem, and lies in the crevices where leek leaves spread, blue in the morning light. I hardly know, now, how much I see and how much remember.

I can see the trees' dark forms, still green, and guess that the beeches' tops are golden, and bouquets of lemon droop among the summer-dark leaves of elms. Hedges carry a crimson birds'-harvest of hawthorn berries, and I do not need to see that in the pastures cobwebs, full of dew, are white until the sun dries them to invisibility.

My ducks sleep in the afternoon on a little plot of lawn beside the orchard, in the shade of Michaelmas daisies, their full crops resting on the grass, their beaks on their backs, their white feathers smooth as new wax candles.

Teeming life is over. There is no urgency for a moment, but an air of fullness, a lull that does not belong to summer, a sense of fulfilment, of triumphant fruition.

At this time of year the sun reaches the west window of the church during Sunday Evensong, settling on the carved grapes and vine leaves at the top of the oak screen, lighting the old gilding and the arches of carved wood: tracery that is kin with the curving branches of the elms outside arching and thrusting up and outwards.

Now the Sexton has no need to light the oil lamps that stand on slender poles at the end of each pew. In winter he lights them before anyone arrives, leaving them turned low to warm up, until, just before the service begins, he shuffles jauntily down the aisle, stiffened by field work, bent a little sideways from long hours of shovelling earth skywards from the bottom of graves. He turns the wicks up, right and left, a bit of an actor, more intent on the gesture than its efficiency, and after he has returned to his seat at the back of the church one or two of the sparse congregation have to reach up and turn down the smoking flames. In winter the atmosphere is warm and homely with the cheerful, indoor smell of burning paraffin, and the warmth revives a sleeping bat who plies from side to side of the shadowy chancel. The lamps do not diffuse much light; each, with a pear-shaped flame, glows alone. Now the atmosphere is sadder, more clearly the ending of the day, as the waning sunlight grows slowly more golden.

Two of the men in the choir are Dick's sons; one of the boys his grandson. His two pretty granddaughters, on one side of the chancel, try to distract the attention of two of the little boys who catch rabbits during harvest, while they sing from hymn books as big as bibles with the other little rabbit catchers on the other side, in well-laundered surplices, their faces shining with soap and soft water.

Half-way through the service, Dick, the incorrigible old Patriarch, downs his first pint at the Tenor Bell. But he will come to the Harvest Festival; and the sheaves of corn and the marrows and pumpkins, onions and apples and carrots and parsnips piling the window-sills, and the plaited harvest loaves, will gain in significance by his presence and the presence of the other old men seasoned and bent in the service of the land.

19

Dick is working to finish the trimming of our lane banks, talking gratefully with any passers-by who give him an excuse for conversation.

'A gentleman in a van asked me where Moor Farm'—or it may be Church Farm or the Old Vicarage—'was to, just now,' he will tell anyone who will stop to listen.

' "Moor Farm", I zaid, "what farm mid that be?" ' No one knows whether he really needs to counter strangers' questions with a question, emphasizing their foreignness, as though he cannot understand what they say.

' "The name's Rackenford," er tol' me. "Oh, Rackenfords'," I zaid. "Why didn' ee says so? Rackenfords' be up over. Nex' place along the lane, like." '

One day, when I was a little girl, walking into the Vicarage for afternoon school, the Doctor called me into his study.

'Lucy,' he asked, 'what is the name of your farm?'

'Church,' I said. 'Church Farm.'

He was disappointed, as he often was by the answers we gave to the experimental questions he tried out on us all; but he soon rallied, saying: 'Well, I've never heard it called anything but Belstones' or Beers', have you?'

'No.'

He had the habit, beloved of children, of talking to them as though they, too, were grey haired; really, I see now, because he was always talking to himself.

'Good.' He twitched his reading spectacles down from

above his eyebrows and looked at me gaily over them, then at the book in his hand. 'There's something here to interest you about the farm Sir Walter Ralegh's father leased, known now as Hayes Barton.' Then he forgot me. 'It belonged to a man named Bartholomew Poer in Henry II's time, and remained in the family, under the name of Poerhayes, until Richard II, when it passed to a family named Duke. But it continued to be known as Poerhayes long after the Dukes owned it, and was subsequently known only occasionally as Dukeshayes. That, in a nutshell, is what this book has to say. Now, the Poers must have owned it for at least two hundred years; and the Dukes, they still owned it in 1584 we know, because in that year Sir Walter wrote to Mr Duke to know whether he might buy it. I wonder how long it was before anyone recognized it as Dukeshayes. For years after the Dukes began farming it, it would have been known as Poers', one may be sure; and as Raleghs' no doubt, long after it had passed out of the hands of Sir Walter's father.'

Poers', Dukes', Raleghs', Beers', Belstones'—whose? Father has been up to the Rackenfords to tell them our plan for Jim and Nancy, so that Robert will not be taken by surprise and can set about finding a new man.

Sometimes I dream that I am walking up to the signpost outside the village, and that I have only a few steps to go before I shall be able to read the directions on its arms. But just before I reach the place the dream shatters.

In the joy of waking, believing the recent months a dream, I hear the cats prowling round the house, their silent excursions betrayed by a creaking sheet of rusty galvanized iron that seesaws under their stealthy feet in a gap in the orchard hedge; and the sharp sound separates truth from fantasy. For that piece of metal has been there for years, always on the point of being cleared away, but now it has become a signal in my landscape of sound, evoking the furtive bodies skulking under the full moon, illumining the moonlit farm, almost all of whose ninety acres spread away under my window: a few fields vigilantly tilled, a few ancient trees and hedges, a stream that dries up in summer, overhung by hazel bushes, a few places which lie in wait to catch the farmer's eye and rouse him from complacency, where crops grow sallow and implements bog down: an infinitesimal piece of a horizon-wide agricultural countryside, individualized by the toil and experience and private reveries of the men who have ploughed their shadows into it.

'Stream field,' Dick will say, 'us drained un the year George were born.' For me, as for the old farm workers, the fields are an anthology of associations: of Richard and me as children, hindering the day's work with our help; of my husband in the fields in his weather-blanched working clothes; of his return, after he had joined the R.A.F. at the beginning of the War, looking amateur in the stiffly new, bulky blue cloth; of the sullen day when we knew that he was dead.

In the daytime all the habitual sounds are as familiar as sights seen every day, and hearing disregards them as sight ignores the verges of a daily trodden road. Only the unusual surprises the wandering mind.

A robin, hunched on a fork, tries out a phrase of his winter song, lingering, wistful, revealing to me, in his music, the yellow leaves in the hedges spiralling slowly downwards, so slowly that they seem to fall on a thread, settling softly on the grass among the few last flowers left on the banks with the castor-shaped seed-cases of campion and the seamed cases of musk mallow seeds; the pasture, grey with moisture, tracked with dark green where the cows have dragged slow feet as they came in for milking; steam rising from the ricks and enfolding the rickyard in silver; the fallen Bramleys in the orchard, hollowed out by wasps who grow drunk, staggering in the wet grass.

Or sometimes an accustomed sound, interrupting the voices of a new season, startles the ear.

House-martins, feeding late young in the nests under the eaves, fill the yard with purring cries, clinging to the walls of nests, or slip, fishlike, through their openings and instantly take to the air again; but their busy voices are out of date.

The cows still dawdle when they are driven in for milking, snatching mouthfuls of grass, stooping and blowing gustily, leisurely. The grass stays good and they are in no hurry for their cake in the shippon—until they reach it, when they will go down on their knees and with grating chains stretch their necks and steal their neighbours' allowance with extended tongues.

Crickets still sing in the hedges, but they, too, are out of tune with the time. From distant farms a new sound answers the shrieking morning chorus of my geese: the quacking and cackling and gobbling of maturing poultry, a loud mutter of hungry ducks and geese, turkeys and crowing cockerels. Their clamour will increase until, a few days before Christmas, it will suddenly be heard no more. The farmers' wives' yearly harvesting will have begun.

21

When I go into a shop in the village I have only to listen, until everyone has spoken, to know who is there, and there is ample time to sort out the company while the local news changes hands. By a procedure of inverted invitation only 'the village' is allowed to share the news. If a newcomer arrives, the customers, one by one, offer her precedence, and if, mistakenly, she declines their offers, the owner of the shop asks for her order.

How heavy money is. While I hold a palmful of coins in my right hand and the forgetful fingers of my left feel for their identity, the weight is exasperating. I use the left hand for sorting because it is the more sensitive, already, through learning Braille.

It is a comfort that all silver has a milled edge; but a penny can collect an edge that feels like milling, too. Sixpences and farthings are the same size. A halfpenny is lighter than a shilling, and a shade bigger. Pennies are lighter than half-crowns. But half-crowns and florins, what of them, when you have not the two to compare? Half-crowns, of course, are bigger; and really it is not my fingers that are stupid, but my mind. Feeling the surface between thumb and second finger while the first explores the edges—copper coins are smoother than silver—only memory fails me when they are laid on the counter, the discarded ones in one pile and the wanted in another. It is lucky that everyone in the shop behaves as though they have all day to spare for the barter of news.

Calling at the cottages in the village, while I was shopping, Father moved from door to door, quietly knocking, to ask for men to help with the potato lifting. No one heard, in the street, what he said at each door, though there was nothing to conceal. When we met he stopped to tell me that there were some, though, he added carefully, not all, who would rather lift potatoes out of gravy than out of the earth, then he went quietly on.

Through the open door of the Tenor Bell a voice drifted on the sunny air in full tide of a story about a cow that had once swallowed a mangold: 'Fine liddle bullick he were, a masterfine milker. "Er'll be off 'is legs in a minute," I zaid, "if you don' send for the vet." My brother rode to fetch the vet; er'd a fine horse to travel. I put the trace horse in the stable; I left the mare in the shafts. The vet had a fine 'and, like a lady's 'and. He put 'is hand gently down the cow's throat. Er felt the mangol', a liddle longways one it were, an' er pulled un up. 'Twas a liddle un as hadn' been chopped.' Unmistakably Dick.

Archie Wrangways, pursuing another theme, seized on the pause. 'Thik garden o' Mowbrays. It ain't never been dug deeper'n a pint mug.'

Partly because it is done after working hours and partly because it is almost the last harvest, there is always a holiday atmosphere about potato lifting. After tea the man who does contract work with farm implements arrives with the spinner hitched to his tractor. A few children always follow him, and with arms working like pistons try to keep up with the men's apparently leisurely movements.

Once I was one of those children, wasting energy in playing and argument while the men, spaced in pairs opposite one another along the spinner's course, straightened stiff backs while they waited, chatting briefly, until the machine came round again. Then everyone stooped, with a sudden burst of speed, their horizon filled with the red earth and the potatoes, creamy and matt, littering its surface, and with arms and legs outspread grabbed the potatoes from the fine tilth, filling baskets which they emptied into sacks leaning against one another in twos and threes on the increasing expanse of bare field empurpled by the setting sun.

Every year some curiously shaped potatoes are thrown up, which even the seasoned little sceptics who grow up on farms cannot resist saving: contorted shapes of human faces or of monstrously formed small animals, which ornament chimney-pieces until they shrivel out of recognition.

At the pay-off there are a few jokes, and the men walk stiffly across the field in the dusk, their jackets slung over their shoulders, and taking their bicycles, propped against the field gate, go off to the Bell.

22

Now the last potatoes are picked up. The Rackenfords have finished their potato harvest, and Jim has finished helping his neighbours with theirs. Father asked him to bring Nancy to see us this evening.

We settled round the table in the kitchen, and immediately the spirit of the place possessed me, as it had on the evening when I broke the news of my receding sight to my father. As a snail's shrinking horns carry inwards its perception I sensed the nearness of the walls, dimly seen, where our shadows recorded our meeting among the invisible imprints of forgotten owners of the farm: walls whose shadowy reticence has never yet been searched by the light of more than an oil lamp or so. In a moment's inward vision the close grey cobbles—laid by men gossiping in the broad accents of Walter Ralegh, and overlaid, years ago, on all the floors except the passage, by effacing cement and again by linoleum and matting—asserted their presence, demanding recognition with the beamed ceiling and the walls that once captured and stilled a measure of moving air and shaped it to the homely atmosphere of our kitchen above the yard growing featureless, now, in the dusk.

On one of the dresser shelves a few books slant one against the other: cookery books of my mother's, one or two books on animal husbandry reaching back to my father's youth, and an anthology of poetry Richard once gave me. Why should they have invaded my mind now with engravings of trussed poultry and game, castle-shaped jelly moulds and an oven called a Conjurer; with photographs of beasts, old-fashioned to unlikeness, with tiny heads and huge flat bodies like sides of beef, halter-led by bearded stockmen; and the unfaltering memory of a poem I thought I had forgotten? It seems, now, that the pictures were no more than a safe-conduct for the poem, for having accompanied it they vanished.

Once Richard and I read the poem, until we knew it by heart, with the luxurious sorrow of inexperience. I have not looked at it since he died, but in memory it might have freed itself at any time; and now it chose to unlatch its words above Father's undertone.

> *When you and I go down*
> *Breathless and cold,*
> *Our faces both worn back*
> *To earthly mould,*
> *How lonely we shall be!*
> *What shall we do,*
> *You without me,*
> *I without you?*

Father had finished telling how our hopes of my carrying on the farm after his death had foundered. He had out the account books, explaining how the money would work out, should they come in with us, to Jim and Nancy, who listened attentively, unemotionally; politeness forbidding any show of surprise or enthusiasm.

> *I cannot bear the thought,*
> *You, first, may die,*
> *Nor of how you will weep,*
> *Should I.*
> *We are too much alone;*
> *What can we do*
> *To make our bodies one:*
> *You, me; I, you?*

In those days, if we took a sideways glance at the thought that one of us would die before the other, we stilled our misgiving with the belief that the one left behind would be supported by the land we had worked together; and in my last hurried look round before my sight dwindled I recognized how the farm has taken the place of husband and child for me: for land that a man has worked as his own holds the memory of him as a child's gesture or a turn of the head will suddenly immortalize the father.

> *We are most nearly born*
> *Of one same kind;*
> *We have the same delight,*
> *The same true mind.*
> *Must we then part, we part;*
> *Is there no way*
> *To keep a beating heart,*
> *And light of day?*

George's unexpected entrance scattered our absorption like a flurry of wind on reflective water.

'I saw you from the road,' he said. 'I thought you would like to see my new ferret.'

He put his home-made ferret box on the table. He had just bought the creature; she was young and unhandled, he explained jauntily.

'Out there, from the yard, you looked as if you were floating in the darkness,' he said, and opened the box.

In the shattered stillness I sensed how the little savage would uncoil, and raise her pointed head, red-eyed, alertly suspicious; and the small boy stand, his hands outspread, his eyebrows vanished under his stiff, fair fringe, his bravado suddenly evaporated.

Nancy leaned forward, like a dreamer, and lifted the ferret out of the box.

'They'm very affectionate, really, poor things,' she said. 'Only no-one loves em.'

We disposed of George, and straightened the books again, but the spell of the moment was broken. Jim must have been wondering, in the silence we mistook for gratitude, how to tell us that they are on the point of giving notice to the

Rackenfords and going away. Why? They are tired, he said, of Nancy being terrified by the neighbours. Sympathy led him back to the speech of his childhood, abandoned now, outside their own home. Terrify, the extravagant local word for tormenting, never came more aptly. They discussed our offer regretfully, for they are not blindly unworldly. When it comes to spending money they can waste it with the best on stuff they have no use for except the advertisers' assurance that they cannot do without it. But that is only decoration. The foundation of their peace of mind demands some other soil.

> *Is then nothing safe?*
> *Can we not find*
> *Some everlasting life*
> *In our one mind?*
> *I feel it like disgrace*
> *Only to understand*
> *Your spirit through your word,*
> *Or by your hand.*

Of course from the moment we are born we are under notice to quit. My father has grown used to incidental leave-takings on the way, and plods along the trodden path of habit assuming that somewhere he will be faced by a dead end. But in the daily work of the farm I have used the round of habitual jobs as rights of way through country where natural features are traced over with the contours of my married life.

> *I cannot find a way*
> *Through love and through;*
> *I cannot reach beyond*
> *Body, to you.*
> *When you or I must go*
> *Down evermore,*
> *There'll be no more to say*
> *—But a locked door.*

23

Mr Luppett called his cows in by moonlight this morning, waking me from my recurring dream of the signpost which I am each time on the point of reading. Listening to our neighbour shouting his daily malison to the beasts on the other side of the valley, I could imagine them rising grudgingly to their feet, crippled with sloth, contemptuous of his threats, unwilling to leave the patch of ground their bodies had warmed on the grey pasture.

A lifetime's repetition fills the mind's eye with such pictures, and at first they compensated for the disappointment following my spoilt dream, for it did not matter whether I could read the directions on the post while I knew from memory what they were. But now that we have no hope of Jim and Nancy coming to the farm I begin to wonder whether the signpost's arms are really blank. And another element has found its way into the disillusion of waking, for confident of reading the directions I walk with assurance in my dream, and wake with intensified awareness of how carefully I have to take every step now. A side-slip or a stumble is more than a momentary set-back: it is a reminder of insecurity, the most disturbing consequence of not seeing.

My surroundings are filled in now by the buzzing hordes of flies that rise from the bloated, watery, over-ripe blackberries in the hedges; by the trembling elder bushes when flocks of chaffinches leave the black-glass berries; by the noise of wagtails in the yard, as they fight for possession of the crests of the roofs, shouting with voices like metal chippings falling on stone. Every spring and autumn a pied and a grey pair fight for mastery, running towards one another with heads and tails flailing, attacking in the air, tumbling and somersaulting with beating wings until, suddenly overtaken by the urgency of nesting or hunting in the furrows behind winter ploughs, they settle down to ignore one another.

Sounds draw attention to days of plenty, and by association hint at autumn's valediction. In a hedge a nuthatch batters a berry stone wedged in a crevice of bark until I believe I see it, perching head downwards, drawing its head back for each hammer blow, raising its wings to steady itself for the forward stroke.

In the early morning at this time of year spiders sit in the middle of newly made and perfect webs in the hedges, hung between nettles and holly and honeysuckle trailers, and between nettles and the ground, each thread of warp and woof magnified by a burden of water: webs which droop heavily, weighted with dew, like sails on a windless day. The day's netting done, the spiders hang in the rigging, their bellies towards the sky, or retire to a cavern of web behind the snare, all on the same motionless watch. In the grass, nets of another kind hang grey between the grass blades: webs of more than one layer, slung by long filaments from the grasses, anchored by crossing cords; basins of thread, like puffs of smoke, each with a sentinel concealed in its shadow.

In the evening the low rays of the sun will light the fleeces of sheep, giving each grey body a halo as it draws the last light of the sun sinking quickly, a red ball for a few moments, disappearing in red cloud. Mist hangs in the copses in the west, all light is reflected to the east where bare trees stand sharply against the sky. And almost at once, before the sunset has gone, there are two lights in the sky: red in the west, and in the east—where the full moon has appeared, the colour of lamplight—the sky is a dome of blue, the ricks bleached silver and the copses sable.

When did I find, for the first time, the air still and quiet after frost, or the leaves of silent trees colourless and grey after a gale? I do not remember matching sight with sound in the past, but these things come back to me now like a language I have learnt long ago and never needed to use, or the key to a locked door—but the lock is broken.

24

Dr Williams returned my last exercise, saying 'Quite perfect. You are beginning very well indeed. How splendid to have such a good memory; never mind whether it is touch or memory in the end.'

Yet in spite of her praise I hardly know what kind of day it has been. Today Dick killed my ducks at my request, and I have plucked them.

Now I shall not hear again their rasping quack as they ask for food, nor their cheerful voices, wheezily quavering, as they follow me to their house to be fed; nor see, in my mind's eye, their smiling faces: for ducks' beaks widen at the top, turning gently upwards where they join the cheeks. Of all poultry they are the most animated, the most jocund.

I have never been able to resolve the paradox of farming, of devoted care leading daily towards the moment of betrayal. Somewhere in my groping after a solution hovers the idea that a price has to be paid for everything. Animals pay a heavy price for man's supremacy. May we remember our debts.

25

It is the time of sales. Father, for whom these provide, with shows and an occasional visit to the Rackenfords, all the entertainment he has or wants, usually goes to one or two. And so, because we are beginning to use our habits as splints for our damaged confidence in the future, we shall take half a day off to go to one.

Dick, whose buoyancy is as little depressed by the makeshift domesticity of his old age as it was by Nurse's genteel housekeeping, will come with us, wearing a Michaelmas daisy tucked above the peak of a sporting black and white checked cap that comes out, slightly crumpled, from the chest under his bed, with the jacket that matches it, and the cord breeches and leggings he wears only for sales, shows, and the races.

'See thik cottage? the liddle un wi' the good thatch? Bill Noakes an' Em lived there, time ago. He were thatcher on Widgery's farm, an' Em were old Widgery's darter, see. Her parents didn' want her to marry un, but er jumped out o' the windy an' there 'twas.'

Every obscure lane that we shall lose ourselves in has been traversed by Dick during his thrashing days, and every farm and cottage we pass finds some matching piece in the jigsaw pattern of his gossip-stuffed memory. Of course he knows the farm we are going to, where 'A Genuine Going Away Sale' is to be held. 'A fine farm, 'twas, when his faither left it to un, 'fore er gambled it away. Times, his mother paid his debts, but er never left off betting. Couldn' help of it, seem so.' He searches for an expression matching his contempt. 'He were a fool to hisself.'

I know the pattern of such a sale almost too well to miss seeing it in detail: the collected implements and gear of farming lined up in a field: horse-drawn ploughs rusted with years of idleness; a tractor which someone has started up so that the engine will fire at a touch when the sale begins; chain harrows, spring harrows and heavy drags; a modern swath turner and side rake; an old horse-drawn tedder that once threw hay into the air and spread it abroad behind the machine; waggons and carts and horse-drawn trailers; a modern trailer with a tractor hitch; piles of horse collars, saddles and traces and bridles, stiff with old sweat, blackened and dull with disuse: two ages of farming laid out before the crowd that will soon move along the field, clustered round the auctioneer like bees round a queen.

The auctioneer and his man with a glue-pot and brush put a dab of glue on the rump of each cow tied in the shippon, and clap on a white disc bearing its number, while early arrivals, leaning on sticks, talk as their finger and thumb close absent-mindedly on a lump of skin by the tail of a beast standing quietly in her stall. As the building fills, the cows fidget their weight from foot to foot and swing their tails, flinging their heads round, with the rattle of a chain, to gaze over their shoulder with liquid eyes at stooping figures who run strange hands down their flanks, feel their udders and pinch their teats, and touch and prod and pinch their skin.

'An honest lot of cows,' the owner says casually to an acquaintance.

Sales begin with an exhortation: the reason why the sale is taking place and why a good price should be paid for everything, followed by a quick recitation of the rules, in the monotone of hocus-pocus, to a congregation that knows it by heart: '... each lot shall be at the purchaser's risk at the fall of the hammer and shall be taken away with any faults or errors of description...' Then, as the sound of the engine of the tractor dies down with its final snort, the auctioneer begins.

'Here is a tractor, Gentlemen, in excellent condition. Who'll bid me seventy pounds for this excellent tractor?'

He looks round, and taps his leggings with his stick. 'Well, say fifty, then. Who'll give me fifty pounds for this tractor, in first-class condition, with a new, reconditioned dynamo?'

Again he stops. The faces that surround him are expressionless. 'Well, start it yourselves, Gentlemen. What will you say for this excellent tractor? Name your price, Gentlemen.'

Someone bids, and the sale starts like a machine.

'Twenty-five, twenty-five, twenty-five.' The auctioneer's glance slides back and forth round the semicircle. 'Thirty, thirty, thirty pounds I'm bid for this excellent tractor with the new reconditioned dynamo.' Now he does not pause until the bidding stops. His voice is like a hammer, and with a slow repetition of the last bid, 'One hundred pounds I'm bid for this lovely tractor; have you all finished, Gentlemen?' he looks once more along the line, then slaps his leggings with his cane. 'One hundred pounds,' he says; and while his clerk takes the name of the buyer he moves on.

In the house the wives pick over the linen, or sit on chairs numbered for the sale. Someone says it is a muddy day for the sale and everyone must bring in a lot of dirt. 'They can't help of it, can em?' her neighbour replies.

The back-chat expected in the opening stages of the sale between rostrum and floor, both imaginary in an open field, will have brought half the crowd here just for the afternoon out, and they are not likely to be disappointed, for they know every auctioneer as children know their teachers.

They know which one will allow the bidding to move conversationally forward, and which will observe, with honeyed sarcasm, 'Gentlemen, we will pause while you talk it over.'

They know which has that revered and heaven-sent gift, an eye for a beast, and the natural geniality that keeps a crowd cheerful when a sale goes on too long and the bidders grow cold and cynical.

And the auctioneer will know them as well as they know

him. Dragging the price of a trailer up by pound rises, he tells one bidder: 'You should give my client a trailer after all the good grass he's let you have.'

The bidder knows what is expected of him. 'Tu my mind it shude be the other way about.'

They wait for old sallies: 'This fork'll stand a lot of leaning on.' 'Getting a price out of you, Gentlemen, is like drawing teeth.' One farmer's wife, invited to start the bidding for a pen of cockerels at a ridiculous price, replies pleasantly: 'See ee in hell, first. Find another fule.'

But this is only an appetizer before the real business: the sale of the cows in the straw-covered yard where a ring of straw-bales has been built with an extra bale where the auctioneer stands with his open catalogue in front of him. Now he never pauses, as the cows, in succession, are driven in and out of the ring. 'Look at this sweet heifer, Gentlemen, out of that wonderful cow,' he reads the name of her dam from the catalogue, 'by that fine bull,' and quotes the resounding title of her sire. 'Look at the blood, Gentlemen. Look at the butterfat. Look at the milk. There's a dairy for you. She'll pay you over and over again.'

The cow moves round in nervous fits and starts, stopping to blow anxiously, seeking an outlet from the ring. The possible buyers, with emotionless faces, wave their catalogues to keep her on the move.

'Well, Gentlemen, what'll you bid me for this really fine cow? Come, Gentlemen, who'll start me? Sixty, sixty, sixty, sixty-two, sixty-two, sixty-two, sixty-four. . . .' While the crowd keeps up a quiet buzz the auctioneer's voice follows a pattern. It is like listening, from a distance, to an unintelligible religious service. The cows, with worried eyes, hurry and stop, move and shrink and look over the barrier. Sometimes a flighty animal will jump the bales. Unperturbed, the auctioneer's voice goes on praising her dam, her sire, her grandam, until she is brought back. 'A sweet and gracious heifer, Gentlemen.'

The last cow disposed of, we move to the piggery, where the merchandise immediately shatters the former almost churchlike solemnity of the ring: sleek, well-brushed sows with noisy, nuzzling litters, active little weaners and fat stores with cunning, ratty faces and restless brown eyes, drowning the auctioneer's voice.

Shrieks break out when anyone touches any young pig, and when the sale is over the noise is almost overpowering as the buyers wheel their trailers in, let their property out of the pens and attempt to mount them on the trailers. Trying to squeeze their bulk into too small spaces, as pigs always will, they jam themselves under trailers or between them, and yell; or, with angry barks, they refuse to move from the pens, while the little pigs are lifted from their confinement, squealing.

As we walk away from the farm a solitary duck swims and quacks on the stream that waters the pastures. (There seems invariably to be a cat or two following accustomed pursuits, or odd poultry that has escaped the collectors, to lend a false air of ordinariness to a day of upheaval.) Noisily she dives, and hunts along the bank, stops to throw water over her back, climbs on to the grass and swallows large morsels. From time to time she raises her head and quacks an enquiry on the autumn-scented air. But her companions are silent in numbered cages at the top of the field.

Dick sleeps all the way home. He has met, as he knew he would, friends he has not seen for years; and he has spent the afternoon, as he expected to, in some quiet hide-out at the back of the inn.

26

While we were at tea with the Rackenfords a man came to the door to ask for a job. Jim has given notice, and they have put it about that they need a man. The newcomer, they said, had lank, long hair, and kept his hands in his pockets while Robert spoke to him. Anne gave him a cup of tea in the back kitchen, running in and out with information.

'I gave un a cup of tea and only one piece of bread and butter twenty minutes ago, and er's not finished yet.'

'As a man eats he'll work,' said my father. 'A slow eater's a slow worker.'

The family all talk Devon among themselves, though the girls, pretty and fashionable, would never do it outside. Both daughters had come to stay for the weekend, and had reverted to their old way of bossing the household with a charming flutter of useless activity, nostalgically stressing the old-fashionedness of their home. One had hung a peeled onion from the main beam of the ceiling to keep the rest from catching a cold that Robert was accused of concealing.

Only Cicely was unexcited. She told me that they had their cows on the hill overlooking the yard and the kitchen window. 'Us couldn't live without a view,' she said, turning towards them lovingly. 'Could you?'

When the girls had gone out of the room, after tea, she told me that Anne is going to have a baby, adding, with placid acceptance, 'Doctors. When 'tis an animal a Vet'inary'll move heaven and earth to help her. Human, you'm treated like dirt.'

This refers to an ancient quarrel her mother had with the doctor who sold the practice to Pamela's father. The doctor, the old lady maintained to her dying day, lost her her first child, a son. My mother told me that until the second boy was old enough to take over a man's work on their farm the loss was referred to as though it were a financial one, and laid at the doctor's door.

27

Now the boys look to their ferreting, and yesterday Peter and Simon and George came to ask leave to hunt our banks, and pressed me to go with them. At some point on our outward journey Dick joined us.

I have never really liked handling ferrets: the stiff hairs of their yellow fur are so living to the touch that they seem to have sensory powers, and now I do not think I could bear the intensity of feeling that would pass between us. But I love the autumn air, the plover rising on rounded wings from the pasture to astonish, in other years, with the white flash of their underwing, as they turn in the blue sky where violet clouds trail mists behind them, and settle again; and hedges, almost bare of leaves, showing through their spears and branches the green fields beyond, with the reflective appearance which will last until next summer.

One day last autumn, going home after a ferreting expedition when the sun was level with the hedgerow trees, I walked across the plough, and looking back after I had crossed, saw that spiders had covered the field with threads slung from crest to crest above the shining, new-cut furrows, and the sun's rays ran along a rippling path of silk, a bright road between me and the sun. But the pleasures of the time of year and the sport have never made me enjoy touching a ferret, though I have always been fascinated by the serpentine body, sneaking along the secret thoroughfares of the animals that live in a hedge bottom, nosing through the dark labyrinth of the burrow.

The boys, noisily admonishing one another to be silent, hunted distractedly for more nets to put over newly discovered holes, jumping off the bank and falling on top of one another, while rabbits escaped from unwatched exits on the unguarded side. Dick leaned out of the hedge on the bank's top. 'You could drive a waggon an' horses along here,' he said; and the zest in his voice conjured up his blue eyes, faded with his person and his clothes, but round and perceptive, and the deep lines of experience carved between the bumpy nose and narrow, squared-off chin; and I thought, inconsequently, that his face would adorn a judge's wig.

On the way back to the house we put the ferret up a tree, the ancient oak in the pasture between whose roots gothic arches lead to the hollow centre, where a family of rabbits lives unmoved by the raid that is made on it at the end of every rabbiting excursion. Even I, alone, at a loss for a dinner, have netted the entrances and put a ferret into this tenement house, where she climbs what one imagines to be decaying stairways, scattering the tenants, some of which, from the sounds within, rush for the attics, while others, never to return, leave by the doorways.

28

A kitten is crying on the mat outside the door, with the short, high mew of one about a month old. Yesterday afternoon one of the mothers called her two children down from the tallet, sitting in the sun, murmuring the low, throaty call of all mother animals who have voices; and a comedy, familiar from its continual repetition, was played out before my guessing eyes.

She would look up at the hay where, from a hole between two bales, the small creatures emerged and paused at the top of the wooden steps. She would turn away and wash her shoulders languorously with long strokes of her tongue, ignoring the experimental efforts of her children, who lacked courage to jump from step to step, but began, instead, to play on the parapet. The mother would pause in her washing and look lazily up at them, while she gave another call, questioning, reassuring. The kittens would make a fresh effort, walking back and forth along the top step, tails erect, stiff legged, trying, occasionally, to reach the next step with their forepaws, but finding they could not, would return to their dalliance.

The mother called for an hour, without vehemence, waiting with the static patience animals command when they are about their own business. At last one would discover that it could jump down one step, and after descending the whole flight with toadlike gathering of hindlegs after fore, would immediately return to the top.

At the end of the afternoon I knew from the silence that both kittens were down, walking stiffly back and forwards under their mother's chin while she brushed them strongly with her tongue as they passed by.

Now one must have made the descent alone, while I worked at my Braille lesson.

The boys read the notes in the printed book to me now, with the symbols for the new letters, and take far more interest in Dr Williams's comments on my work than they ever express on the results of their own.

'I say, Lucy's got "Perfect" this time.'

'That's nothing. Once she got "Quite Perfect". You weren't there.'

Dr Williams's instructions are read out in reproving, dictatorial voices. ' "You have to keep your reading finger square with the line, and move horizontally along it. Try not to move it up and down more than you can possibly help." '

The criticisms intended for them they read in a consolatory tone. ' "Yes, I know that it is always a snag when one is not left entirely to oneself: it is mistaken kindness, though, isn't it? Please tell them from me that however hard, they should try to leave you to read from touch. It is much more fun, for one thing, and, for another, they are really detaining, instead of helping you." ' For with each exercise I send a letter, and once told her how hard it is for the boys, with the printed answer in their hands, not to hurry my searching finger with broad hints.

Lingering over their departure they look for some piece of news, or failing that invent an invitation.

'Are you coming to our fireworks, Luce?'

'Of course, if you'd like me to.'

'Oh yes.' Doubtful about answering a direct question, they reassure themselves. 'You're livelier than some old ladies we know.'

Every year Tom helps them to build a huge fire of hedge cuttings and old tyres, on one of the few occasions when he takes time off from gainful toil. The children run about with sacks over their shoulders to keep them warm, waving torches of rag soaked in old sump oil blazing on the end of sticks, moving with grotesque attitudes against the firelight, stooping to rekindle their lights and pull charred, half-baked potatoes out of the fire, raising the scent of the dying year in the wet leaves disturbed in the tufted grass.

Their bought fireworks are always expended during the first few minutes of darkness. Lavish spending is discouraged by their parents, and frugality encouraged to the extent of seizing birthday and Christmas presents of money sent by relations, to put towards a new tractor, a van, or an electricity plant.

The year is groping from autumn to winter with the sound of the earth sucking, of moisture dripping off trees, and the thud, night and day, of acorns falling heavily on to the roofs of sheds.

Raw days follow gales and rain, when autumn leaps forward into winter. Then there will come a hot, golden day that streams back into summer. Only the stillness, the lull that does not go with summer days, brings back to mind the time of year. Or a sound: a blackbird's stutter as it flies out of a hedge, a gull's derisive cry among the flock that heads towards some scene of winter ploughing, homing starlings rushing overhead with the directness of a shoal of fish, or plovers' heavier sound of wings.

Frosts hard enough to lay thin ice in cart ruts bring down the last leaves with a continuous rustle, and sharpen the voices of owls at night, until I know that in the moon's white brilliance the oaks cast long shadows on the pasture, and in the sun-drenched days that follow, the northern shade of hedges will stay white.

Or there is fog at night, and the beam of a torch cuts through its moving surface, a round beam, full of swimming particles of moisture, which fans out to rest on the heifers asleep in the rick-yard with their forelegs bent under them, and the flock of geese who slide away from the light with heads erect and quick, pattering feet. A calf sleeps in her deep bed of straw at the back of her pen, the ferret in her round nest in the hay in her night house. The hens, roosting on the beams in the barn, rock as they stretch their necks to look over curved beaks bending towards me. On nights like this we smell our own wood smoke in the yard, and I see it all in mind as clearly as though it were noonday.

30

In winter the kitchen regains the hold on the farm which was lost in summer when everyone was out in the fields. Now interest bends inwards. Fine rain falls steadily, almost imperceptibly, while the spongy pastures soak, slowly bleaching. Water drips noisily off gutters and runs loudly down pipes into full tanks. Dick spins out his working hours to shorten his solitude at home and to ensure a week's dinners, lingering in the kitchen after he has brought logs in and stacked them to dry, rummaging among the lumber in his junk-store of reminiscence for some tale to keep him by the fire.

''Twas a day like this Bill Yeo zaid he were going to shoot Ernie Luppett.'

'Said he'd what?'

'Shoot un.'

Dick is far too experienced a story teller to betray his art in animation, and answers laconically. But he stands, by chance, with his back to a chair, and when he knows that I shall listen he folds himself stiffly into it.

'Time ago, Bill had the farm next to Ern Luppett's, an' rented a bit o' land from a London gentleman, a few acres the gentleman thought one day er'd build a house on. Well, Ern bought the land without telling Bill, I don't know the ins an' outs, but I went with Ern the first time er asked Bill for the rent. He were a bit nervous, like; Bill'd a temper like a saucy bull.

'Bill come straight to the point, how er wished er had a gun, to shoot Ernie. But just before that er zaid a most interesting thing. Er told Ern er could show un ten thousand pound any day. Then er zaid er'd like to shoot un.

'That evening I stayed an' had tea with Ernie, an' 'twas drip, drip, drip, off the roof all the time. Ernie sot with his 'aid in 'is hands.

' "What's up, Ern?" I zaid. "Worried about Bill? I don' expect er'll shoot ee, really."

' "Here," Ern zaid, "did you hear what Bill zaid about being able to show me ten thousand pound? Do ee think 'tis true?"

'He were very thoughtful all the evening.'

On these moist, warm, sunless days, when the rain ceases, copses and fields are folded in mist which hangs in woods between the trees. Flocks of chaffinches move along the hedges, a flock of starlings is never far away, on the fields or whistling and purring in trees with a sound like kisses. In this veiled weather I feel the character of trees: the outward thrust of oak, the upthrust of elm until the branches droop gracefully, mournfully, the beeches' feathered outline traced in straight twigs, ashes whose branches curve downwards until they raise their knotted tips towards the sky.

In this climate of steamy air and soft cloud I still remember how the sun breaks through to lighten some small patch of land isolated in mist: a flock of gulls on a green field, a stretch of red plough, a cluster of silver ricks, the pasture oaks whose branches suddenly cast a shadow on their lichened, deeply furrowed trunks. Mistle-thrushes sing in the hedges with robins and wrens, until the mist thickens and trees have no shape in the clothing atmosphere and birds only chatter in the hedges.

Every morning, long before it lightens, cockerels raise their voices, louder than ever during their youthful summer, all crowing, then are silent. I have fed my geese in the goosehouse instead of in the open. After some cajoling and driving they went into the house; the poor things cannot guess that this is to accustom them to the house again before they are shut up next week, when they will be killed.

31

Geese are easier to pluck than ganders. Father and Dick and Nancy and I sat on a ring of straw-bales in the barn with a softly moving pile of feathers growing at our feet. Like men at a sheep shearing we hardly spoke, and for the same reason: wandering attention leads to the injury of delicate skin, and the worker's loss of pride.

During the morning Archie Wrangways joined us, and then he and Dick joined together in old men's recollection, but even that was muted, stirring our tranquillity no more than the flakes that lingered off our hands to join the mass lying lightly on the floor.

Archie had lost a pick—a two-pronged fork. Speculation as to how it had gone followed, and it was clear that both of them were sure who had taken it. With no fuel for argument an elegy was begun. It has been a good pick, with a slender stem, light, too, and well balanced. A pick's a useful thing. Then the theme divided and one defended the thief, unnamed, and the other retorted that he'd feel differently if it had been done to him. But the first stuck out that you shouldn't blacken a man's name on speculation, and pressed his point with an allegory: 'You can have a good dog called Fido. Call un Gypsy you might as well shoot un.'

Sometimes Dick, unable to bear our silence, rallied Nancy with a provocative remark: 'Thik kitten you give me, Nance, it ain't a tom, 'tis a liddle maid.' And Nancy, with studied innocence, responded: 'I'm sure 'tis a tom, it had a tom's face,' so that Dick could reply, sedately: "Tain't their faces you tell em by.'

Nancy's kitten has turned up for years, like the fox that Mr Luppett resuscitates every time anyone loses any fowls to one. We know how he looked out of his window at dawn, 'time ago' (one might suppose a month), 'and saw a little brown gentleman that sot in the hedge by the fowl house'; how he told his missis to bide and keep an eye while he fetched his gun; and we are told with multiplying detail the size and colour of the fox he shot. Mr Luppett has been a widower for ten years.

But the kitten has made its last appearance. Dick's joke needs Nancy for a foil, and she is going away at the end of the month. On New Year's day Jim will start work on a Sussex farm.

Leaving our work stiffly for our regular jobs and returning, we plucked twenty-five geese by dusk, thoughts from opposite poles meeting in our brief conversations: how these were nice birds, plump and well finished, averaging what? twelve pounds? Of how goslings are sociable creatures, bandying opinions round a bowl of water, answering human voices, earning themselves names: Shorty, Flatfoot, Dopey, Tim. Of how deliciously the rich skin would brown if a little flour were dredged over it before the final basting; of how goslings raised by their own mothers are never so tame as those fostered by hens, as though geese taught their children to be suspicious.

Such divided feelings, shared, probably, by all farm people with sympathy for animals, aired among us every year at the plucking, furnished, for me, the familiar picture of the frost of down settling on our hair, our clothes, on the cats who crossed the barn on business and stayed to watch; on the tattered banners of dusty cobweb hanging from the beams, thickened like fine cloth by clinging meal, moving softly; on the wide-brimmed, extravagant straw hat left hanging on a nail years ago by some forgotten haymaker.

Now the two goslings that are being kept for our Christmas dinner, and for Nancy's and Jim's, walk about the farm with the stock geese in silence, stealthy and watchful, as I have seen birds in other years, with necks outstretched. From time to time one of them calls for its former companions, otherwise they are mute, bewildered, and suspicious of the absence of their friends.

I used to shut my geese up for fattening three weeks before Christmas, and once, while Dick was taking away the first batch for sale, one of those we were keeping for ourselves escaped. Walking slowly across the small field by the goosehouse, languidly looking round, when she reached the bank she flew over it and dawdled through the yard to the pasture where she used to graze with the flock. There she stood silently staring across the deserted meadow grizzled with moisture, under a neutral sky.

At the time I thought that that was how a returned prisoner might stand and look, half unbelieving, at his home, reality less substantial than remembrance; and the strange little scene stayed in some corner of my mind to emerge now with a meaning that escapes enlightenment, but which hints at the falsehood of a cherished idea that all would be as before, if one could only find the way back to the time when everything went well.

32

A few days before Christmas the country grows quiet. On the farms all but the laying and stock birds have gone, and the demanding voices of ducks and geese, turkeys and cockerels, raised since autumn in a strident morning and evening clamour, are stilled.

Christmas Day is the farmwife's Harvest Thanksgiving, and after Church neighbour boasts to neighbour of the head of poultry she has dressed and sent away. It is also the one day in the year when a truce is observed in the age-old tug-of-war between human ingenuity and the adroitness of animals to obstruct the aims of husbandry.

There must be very few farms where the stock is not given an indulgent measure of feed, a more lavish share of bedding, in honour of the day, without an eye to profit. And so, because of the circumstances of Christ's nativity, a farm is an inspiring and satisfying place at Christmas. Tomorrow the battle will be on again; men will exploit beasts to the limit that Nature will tolerate, and animals will thwart their intentions with every strategy of obstinacy and passive cross-purpose in their means.

In the late Christmas afternoon Father and I walked round the high fields. From the moist pasture feeding plover rose with their seashore cry to settle again a few feet away; flights of starlings swept over with a rustle of silk; blackbirds raised their fierce evening chatter, and wrens their sunset voices like whirring alarm clocks: the curfew sounds of any winter evening.

I have wondered, sometimes, whether without knowing that it was Christmas Day one might go out and sense its significance, perhaps find some trace of the miraculous. But on our homeward journey, while an owl cried and the day birds were silent, the sun sank as enigmatically as it had lit the day.

The legend of the cattle kneeling at midnight on Christmas Eve that Thomas Hardy knew is still familiar to the old people, though it is brought out in the half-sceptical disguise that masks their telling of ghostly tales and the uses of charms and spells.

So fair a fancy few would weave
In these years! Yet, I feel,
If someone said on Christmas Eve,
'Come, see the oxen kneel

In the lonely barton by yonder coomb
Our childhood used to know',
I should go with him in the gloom,
Hoping it might be so.

33

Sometimes, during the days that follow Christmas, if winter has come early it is inclined to relent.

On a soft day in the dying year Cicely came to tea, possibly to cheer me up because she knew that Jim and Nancy had been to say goodbye. Mrs Eastcott is going with them. They are to live on a housing estate no great distance from the coast or from London. Whatever will the old lady make of it! Nancy's regrets are offset by excitement; for all the disturbance Jim shows he might be going to Exeter for the day. No prospects seem to dazzle him, and no doubts undermine his composure. He was born moderate, and he stands on the middle of a seesaw, balancing Nancy's sky-high expectations against her mother's doleful prophecies.

Cicely brought a bowl of cream, as she always does, saying, 'Folks don't know how to make cream these days.'

They had killed a pig for Christmas, salting down all that they had not needed for fresh meat.

''Twas priddy liddle pork,' she said. ''Twasn't a big pig, an' 'twas priddy liddle pork.' By the pleasure in her voice I could imagine her handling it affectionately, the joints pink and covered with pearly fat.

We had tea in the sitting-room at the back of the house, the gentleman's side, with the front door facing the fields which some owner with grand ideas once planted with chestnut trees, carefully spaced, as though it were a park.

'This part of the house would have been nice for your

parents to retire to if. . . .' Evidently she was going to say 'if your mother and Richard were alive,' for she stopped, and finished indefinitely, 'if things had worked out differently.'

We talked a little about the hopes Father and I had had of Nancy and Jim coming to the farm, and of the reason why they had decided not to, then of happenings on both farms. She said one of their cows had been got down and 'hornged' by the others. She used the word several times, sounding the 'g' as though she said hinged. She had just been to see one of her neighbours who has had a baby, a daughter born some years after the tail-end of her family.

'Er'll just be ready to be useful by the time the maiden ahead of she marries.'

Cicely, who loves children, regards them in the old-fashioned way, as one of the assets of a farm; and in every direction her ideas have been shaped in a mould that time has shattered. She is not so much odd as remote. Local hearsay supposes that she is able to bless away ringworm and warts, and once, with the bravado of childhood, I asked her how it was done. 'Ah, I can't remember,' she said. When I appealed to old Robert, her husband, he said he did not know, but not to seem unkind, added: 'A man must tell a man and a woman a woman. But I expect they'm cured somehow else.'

We turned back to Nancy's trouble, and Cicely murmured something about seeing what could be done. Then, because I cut the cake, the drift was lost: the seed cake, made with too much care, deceptively risen and baked golden, was a hollow shell.

'You need someone to live with ee,' Cicely said. Then, evidently considering that she might have hurt my feelings by blaming my lack of sight, she added: 'You put too much fat in it,' and her usual rider, 'folks don't know how to bake, these days.'

34

New Year's Eve and a night full of stars, a brittle coat of ice on the puddles in the yard, frost in the pasture as bright as the sky, sharpening the voices of the owls. At eleven a peal of bells echoed the light in the sky: crowding bell notes under crowding stars. The ringers rang with pauses until just before midnight, finishing with a single bell. At the year's beginning the bells clashed out again, reeling and bucketing, pelting downhill.

I know by heart the grey-green dawn of a frosty day: the flush over the trees in the east, the sun rising, round and red, behind the oaks, shooting the sky—waved like sand when a calm sea has ebbed—with sea-shell colours behind the naked beauty of oak and ash spears in the easterly hedges, though I have never caught the moment when the red sun turns white. Since I was quite a child I have had work to do at this time of day. But when the sun has cleared the oaks the light of day begins.

Pastures that hissed and gurgled yesterday underfoot are crisp, with sharp edges to the cattle hoof marks. Only the bell-notes of tits defy the weather, the other birds do not sing, but vent angry cries: the shriek of a jay, the jealous voice of a mistle-thrush. Larks get up from the stubble with cries like creaking saddle leather, a flock of chaffinches reluctantly leaves a hedge. Birds do not fly eagerly, but low and unwillingly as though stiffened by cold, and crouch, torpid, in hedges.

Yet, by next day, all frost has thawed. The plover in the pasture are feeding with a flock of starlings, the plover making their wounded cry, the starlings a sound like water running over pebbles. I can tell, by their voices, what they are at: for starlings, exulting while they feed, fly voiceless, their movement betrayed by a rush of wings; and feeding plover rise singly, with a single cry, and sink a few feet away, but when a flock of plover lifts, the birds wheel and turn with many voices, and I see in memory their continuous movement, like flakes or feathers hanging in the still air.

The wagtails protest on the roof-tops, disturbed from the dung-heap by men laying rubble beside it for a firm entrance to the yard. And while the refuse of red clay and straw and cow-hair—the remains of demolished cob houses—is pressed into the mire of the gateway where cows have churned up the mud, Dick, lending a hand to the contractor's men, falls into irresistible reminiscence.

'Cob walls'll fall down for a pastime if you don't keep their 'aids an' their feet dry. Stones at the foot an' thatch on top they *got* to have. I've seen cottages without roofs ploughed in where they stood, in my lifetime.'

It is a perfect winter day, without hint of spring or memory of autumn, still and quiet; trees, without movement, will be wrapped in the meshed shadow of their branches.

35

Like my mother, I spring-clean in the New Year, before tilling demands a comfortable house for a tired man to come back to in the evening. Turning out a chest this morning, in the hit-or-miss fashion I have to use, but managing fairly well, I came across an old notebook in which my mother had recorded the quantities of food necessary for parties, and I kept it out for Father to read to me at dinner time.

'1 lb. of butter to one fourteen inch loaf will make thirty-five to forty slices of bread and butter.
$\frac{1}{2}$lb. of tea will make one hundred cups.
1 lb of coffee will make one gallon of black coffee. . . .'

The quantities must have gone back to Mother's youth and the great Harvest Homes and Sheep Shearings when all the neighbouring farmers joined together, with their men, for successive days on one another's farms. Richard used to delight in these tables of quantities when he was a little boy, staying with us in the school holidays, egging her on with questions about how many helpings she could cut from a leg of lamb or a saddle of mutton, how many pounds of potatoes would be needed to feed twenty people. The largeness of her ideas seemed to appeal to him like poetry. And while he sat on the chair by the fire with the tabby cat hugged against his rabbit-ribs, fringing the cat's fur between the fingers of one hand, she would feed his taste for expansive ideas with scraps of her experience, serialized, talking to him as though he were a young man, about to set up in farming and, of course, married.

'If your wife's not a farmer's daughter—though I strongly advise ee to marry one—she'll have to broaden her ideas. She must go to sales and pick up big dishes. When she cooks hams she'll need them. And she'll need big kitchen tables, not many folks want em, now; you can pick em up for ten shilling. Er'll need em for haytime and corn harvest and thrashings in winter. Er must learn to think big.'

With my mother the farm always came first, and she would find warnings in the establishments of gentlemen-turned-farmers, talking broader as she warmed to her subject.

'Mrs Somebody's going to have another chiel. 'Tis a pity er's going to have another so soon. She've enough to do, keeping her men fed and warm.' 'Mr Somebody's all right at Latin and Greek, seem so. Could spout they for a pastime. But have ee ever zeed un trying to lay a hedge?' And she would turn her dough and slam it down on the table with energy intensified by the idea of an inexperienced man grappling with the sprawling branches of an overgrown hedge on a bank top.

In return, Richard used to tell her about his life in London, of the gang-games and battles of the streets, in which he and his friends worked off their energy; or about the time when he was a very little boy, still able to play with the girls, when they used to make grottoes, in spring, of stones and little bits of anything green or flowering they could find, and arrange them on the edge of the arid South London pavements, and ask for 'a penny for the grotto' from passers-by; though he was really forbidden by his parents from joining in the money-making, as he was from the extortion of 'a penny for the Guy' in the autumn. But there was so little else to do out of doors, and somehow the money-making lent a touch of adventure and a sense of achievement to the pastime, with hazy thoughts of making a fortune.

I think my mother understood Richard's craving for expansion; certainly she appreciated his delight in farming, and so she talked to him endlessly while she worked, her implements neatly ranked beside her on the spotless table, moulding her dough into apple pies, with even the cut-off rind of the fruit making orderly curling patterns where they had fallen, and he hugged the cat by the fire.

Her life was ordered by a routine as accurate and dovetailed as a nurse's; and all the time she worked she knew, by the signs that she saw in the yard from her overlooking window, just what was going on. Nothing happened that she was not aware of, though once, when Richard asked her something about tillage, she replied, scornfully, that she did not know. To her mind a farmer's wife taking part in outside work, except tending calves and fowls, was as incongruous as a parson's wife taking to preaching.

She must have been a lovely girl: fair and finely built, with the fresh complexion and white, even teeth that give a joyous impression of health and strength. Age did not bow her, and she never grew fat; she remained, always, capable and good looking. Sometimes, before my sight failed, I used to be ashamed of Nancy's help because my mother had none. But times have changed; for pleasure, as well as from Father's necessity, I have always helped out of doors.

Every day, before breakfast, my mother did the housework. Her life, like the life of other farmers' wives, was a continual battle against dirt: dirt brought in on the men's feet, red marks where their arms rested on tablecloths, and earth-stains on shirts and overalls and towels and the sheets which, in spite of Father's noisy ablutions, by the end of the week were faintly red. During wet weather implements carried mud into the yard, already muddy, and the stuff came in on our feet; in dry weather it drifted in as dust. It was all swept away, and on Mondays the washing was well on the way to being hung out, before we sat down to our porridge and cream and piled plates of bacon and eggs and fried potatoes. After that, she cut more rashers off one of the joints that hung in linen bags with the hams and shoulders on the hooks in the ceiling beams, and put them in the larder for the breakfasts of the next day. One day each week she interviewed the grocer, sitting at the kitchen table while she made good the deficiencies in the reserve store-cupboard—that from which the everyday store-cupboard was replenished.

She never cooked dinner only for us. As long as I can remember, Dick came in, and often extra men lent by neighbour farmers at busy times in return for help Father and Dick gave them. At one o'clock a fine, solid dinner appeared on the table. When visitors came no change was made: we might have chicken and apple tart and cream, but we had them on other days, too. Callers were not made to feel like visitors, and they went home as they were meant to, knowing that Church Farm lived well. One funny little quirk my mother had: ladies were never offered a second helping. Occasionally someone lent a landgirl to help, and naturally, after working as hard as the men, she was equally hungry. But politeness forbade her asking for more, and when, as was inevitable, her comments later reached me, passed on to my mother they made no difference.

Every afternoon an enamel basin containing about half a gallon of milk, with the cream risen, was put on the stove to scald—the cream smooth as paint until, on the low heat, it crusted and wrinkled, then richly cracked, and finally rose into what would have been bubbles if it had not been taken off then to be stood until next day.

Sometime during the day Mother skimmed the cream that had been scalded the day before. Twice a week she made butter, and baked cakes so that she would have 'something to cut at' if anyone called or delivered anything. At four she put a pot of tea on the warm side of the stove and a cake on the table so that everyone could help themselves. At six she gave us tea: bread and butter and jam, pasties or ham and eggs, some kind of closed tart and cream, and the unchanging fruit-cake. After washing up she put next morning's porridge in the cool oven, and went to bed at nine.

That was an ordinary day: no jam-making, bottling, or bacon-curing. No excursions to the harvest field with cans of tea and baskets of cake. No unexpected callers: seedsmen, dealers in animal medicines, inspectors of this and that, advisers, mechanics, or the vet.

What distinguishes a farmhouse from any other country house? Sometimes I wonder, now that the certainty, once lightly accepted, of living out my days in one has slipped away. The difference is so clear, and yet, because I have taken it for granted for a lifetime, so evasive. But it would be obvious immediately, I believe, to any stranger who arrived, if it were possible, without seeing the evidence outside: the oil-drums and implements, the miscellaneous timber and old iron lying about even in our tidy yard, the henhouses and coops, old shafts, drainpipes and rolls of wire: the junk that one day might turn out to be just what one is looking for.

The conversation in the house is all farm, but there is something else that identifies it too, a special vitality: the bacon hanging from the ceiling is a reminder of hurrying days of cutting up and salting during the past winter; the wide table in the kitchen, where substantial meals are prepared and eaten, is there also for the dozens of plucked fowls that are dressed, and piles of trays of eggs that are washed and packed every evening, ready for the van that calls weekly. One wall is lined with mackintoshes, coats, gloves, and the collection of jackets that anyone but a farmer would call worn out, but which are ready to replace the soaked garments changed, sometimes, several times a day. Lanterns and matches and torches stand on a shelf above them, to remind town visitors that once inside in the evening there is small certainty that the master will stay there.

In the larders cakes and bacon and cheese and extra bread wait, seldom in vain, for callers. Cooking seems to be always going on, about to begin, or just concluded, for meals that must be on time, or the men, seeing no cloth on the table when they come in, will stand about dejectedly or irritably, according to their turn of mind, thinking of the bit they might have been doing. And all the time the missis knows what is going on outside. The house is the hub of the farm's universe.

During three fog-muted days my surroundings have made their presence felt in the breath of the day on my face, the subtle quickening and smothering of sound as the fog lifted and fell. It is at times like this that I most dread the prospect of leaving the farm, for its walls are sounding-boards and its paths hand me on from one landmark to another.

All the first day the mist thickened, creeping up like a tide until it covered the orchard, isolating trees standing distant and reserved, subduing the birds to curt phrases. At dusk it seemed to grow lighter while the white blanket pressed against the windows, stifling the sound of the tractor coming into the yard for the night.

George came in the evening to fetch his cat, which has been making trouble with our tribe. It came to meet him with an effusive display of purring and ingratiation. 'Poor chap, he got lost in the fog,' George said. 'He's come to forgive himself.'

During the night the creeping mass grew still, and in the morning the sun rose secretly above it, discovering, at last, my head and face while I stood in a calm sea.

By the middle of the morning the fields lay in sunshine: the lane would be filled with blue shadows where the cows puffed cloudy breath while they dawdled to a far pasture, Dick's gruff admonishments behind them piercing the bright air.

Down the lane, Mr Luppett talked to Father over the

hedge, leisurely in the sunshine, beside his old mare shifting her feet comfortably while she waited in the shafts.

'Keep a winter's muck in hand and put un out in the fall. Ah,' he added, after repeating this piece of his mind several times, 'then, if you have a long October, you can get it out while the land's dry. Keep a winter's muck in hand.'

A long October. Poet Luppett, you invoked days of mild sunshine on silvered fields, and flights of gulls and plover and rooks and rocking wagtails following the plough, and your mare in her winter coat spiked with mud, blowing smoke while she waits in the shafts of a richly laden muck-cart, the ploughland steaming.

At dusk the fog crept back, gently sheeting a perfect winter day.

It was still against the windows next morning. I sat over a morning cup of tea, enclosed, with the rustling firelight and softly settling logs, against the blanketed day. The silent fog wrapped the room with a feeling of intimacy, a sense of being alone in the world, quite different from the kitchen's bright contrast, on other winter days, with rain or wind outside. I lit a lamp to compensate for the doused light of the day, and remembered a conversation with Nancy when the lamp was lit and she began to talk with the responsiveness of a singing bird in a shaft of winter sunshine.

'What would you think if you had a nice Dining-room Suite in here, but you hadn't paid for it?'

'I should be miserable,' I said.

'So would I,' she agreed, regretfully, mistaking my meaning.

I thought of the dignified ladder-back chairs and the dresser with its brass handles, the scrubbed kitchen table: the unchanged kitchen of at least two generations, and had no comfort from the conclusion that since Nancy and Jim are not coming to the farm no such invasion by modish Suites will take place. For Nancy's talk of Companion Sets, Suites, and Duchess Sets—she picks up her terms from catalogues and magazines—would bring animation to the house whose vitality is ebbing away. And anyway she is far too sturdily rooted in tradition to do anything really drastic; quite small gestures to modernity would satisfy her: a mere Duchess Set here, a Companion Set there, whatever they may be.

For about an hour the fog lifted and there was a burst of birdsong: robins and mistle-thrushes, and the great tits' flinty cry, 'teacher, teacher teacher'. Then it billowed up again.

'It do drift in fleeces across the white face o' the sun,' said Dick, and hobbled away, shamefaced at his own expressiveness; and the birdsong ceased.

37

A French girl is staying at the Old Vicarage for the school holidays. To teach the boys French? Unlikely. To learn English, and pay for it? More likely. To help on the farm? Perhaps all three. Experience suggests that Pamela and Tom would not undertake anything that did not benefit the farm. But Hélène knows how to take care of herself.

I had tea with them on my way to the Mowbrays—it was the Judge's ninetieth birthday—and Hélène asked to come with me.

The Mowbrays had finished tea, but the tray had not been taken away and they insisted on each of us having a large slice of the birthday cake they would never finish by themselves. They were delighted with Hélène, who was charming and demure. Mrs Mowbray drew her into a chair beside her; if she had heard my introduction she overlooked it.

'What's your name?' she asked.

Hélène used the boys' abbreviation. 'Nell,' she shouted.

'Nell,' said the old lady. 'Little Nell.' Unable to connect her with any of their widespread acquaintance, she hit on a happy alternative: 'Someone of that name in Shakespeare.'

As always, the cat was mumbling cake on the table with a noisy show of fastidiousness. From sounds of fidgeting I knew that all the dogs impaled us on their gaze while we ate ours.

Hélène politely ventured into conversation, carefully choosing her words. 'Of what breed are the two large dogs?'

'Hounds. Foxhounds,' the Judge told her gently.

She made a further effort. 'Their tails wave nicely.'

'Sterns,' said Mrs Mowbray.

On the way home we congratulated one another on our despatch in polishing off birthday cake on top of the tea we had already had. Hélène said she had given most of hers to the dogs.

How in the world, I asked, had she persuaded them to leave her alone after that?

She replied, serenely, that she had stuck her fingers up their noses.

38

North-east wind and sunshine in a sky pale as summer, and ice cracking glassily in the wheel-ruts. It is not a fierce wind, rather a cold air that sets the last leaves of oak saplings hissing with a constant, brittle murmur, as though each leaf spun in the bitter air.

On such a day the sun will set black: black cloud over the Moor, black hedges lining colourless fields. Yet, when I went to fetch vegetables from my garden, I heard wrens hunting in the hedges, flitting from branch to branch, busy as mice, and I heard the geese beginning to be amorous, ducking in puddles in the yard and preening; the gander would be stretching with loudly flapping wings, straddling on short legs. And while we were busy in the house, Dick, for no reason that I can remember, when he carried in the logs, conjured indoors the hectic, golden days of harvest time: 'If any machinery broke down then Harry's old man's hat would be over the horse pond.'

Harry's old man, Nancy's grandfather, a tenant farmer, had the same irascible temperament as mine had, with an added inheritance of eccentricity which he handed on, undiminished, to poor Harry, who found it too unwieldy to fit into the softened, politer time of his generation. But it passed, a generation before, as character; and I sometimes wonder how much of Harry's queerness would have been accepted as mere temperament in days gone by.

I used to think I would like, above all things, to sit by a

wood fire over breakfast, watching a frosty sunrise. (It is not possible to watch the sunrise from our kitchen window, and anyway we have always been too busy to linger over breakfast.)

I was thinking, then, of a kindly white frost, the sun rising behind the hedge elms to recapture the frosted fields, until, in the midday warmth, an owl might call from the Vicarage trees and a pigeon reply; not the colourless, freezing cold of today, that blackens trees and hedges in the sunrise and the stream of water freezing as it runs away from the dairy; that sets the moisture at the lane's edge like black glass, and the crests of ploughland like metal. In weather like this the birds that do not sing all day betray themselves only by soft, crackling sounds in the hedges, and the plover call restlessly as they settle querulously for the night.

In the silence of a calm white frost, if a man hammering in the village bangs his thumb or grazes his hands chopping kindling, what he says is carried slyly, on still air, across the neighbouring countryside. Men in the fields listen to the barrels rolling off the brewer's truck outside the Bell, the schoolchildren rush out to play at mid-morning in a ball of noise, like a distant swarm of bees, until a thaw restores village privacy and the country's seclusion, with hissing pastures, dripping gutters, and sudden pattering showers when over-burdened trees let fall their load of moisture.

39

Pigs can see the wind, Nancy once said. I asked her how she knew. Everyone says so, she replied. We had been out to my garden, and in the distance fields were veiled in moving vapour as though the wind were visible.

A westerly gale beat on the house then, as it has today, roaring through trees, obliterating every other sound. None of the cats has dared to cross the yard; the older ones knew from experience that the wind would sweep them aside as they left the buildings.

Now there is a full moon, and the gale is stilled. An owl cries. A heifer that has strayed from a field picks her way among latticed shadows in the lane, and pausing, lows. A duck quacks loudly and is silent.

Seeing, in mind, as clearly at night as by day, the invisible night suddenly belongs to me.

40

Fine rain, drifting off the Moor with the density of smoke, whirls and eddies in the yard. The wet wind gets under mackintoshes, curling round us as soon as we leave the shelter of the buildings.

A postcard came from Nancy with a picture of the front at Brighton, but no information except that they are well and she hopes we are. She has no experience of writing news; all that has been expected of her in the past is an assurance of her safe arrival. Something about the weather and this souvenir of sightseeing reminded me of a day a year ago when a Muscovy drake and duck appeared in the yard.

They stood almost silently, speaking only in undertones. They did not quack; the drake opened his beak and whispered the shape of one. He had a solemn bearing; his plumage was white and dark green with a purple sheen, his head was hoary—grey and warty—and his eyes were brown. He stood, bowing his head now and then, in soundless conversation. She was gay, in a modest and matronly way. The feathers on her back were dark green, but her head and breast were pure white. She looked as though she had gathered a shawl over her head and across her breast, and she bustled about, dumpy and admiring, then returned to her mate to hear his whispered comments. Her eyes were round and blue, and she cast her glance obliquely upwards to look at the buildings.

When they had considered the yard, and had bowed to the

geese—who took no notice—and to the cats who were gingerly picking their way through the mud, they went home up the lane, she walking briskly a little ahead, with her shawl gathered round her, he more slowly, stretching his neck to speak occasionally. One could see that they had been married for years.

 # 41

The brilliance of moss defies the sleep of winter with a strong, damp, earthy, living smell that is raised at a touch and brings to memory the feathered arms of brightest, lightest green mantling wet banks, and forests of small moss flowers like diminutive conifers, and luxurious cushions of green plush. Among them lichens grow, ashen-coloured, with little cups on stems.

In wet weather lichens of seaweed growth will cover the bent and gesticulating cider-apple trees in fur like green frost, with another like dusty hair. On dry days they silver the trunks of oaks in the sun.

There is yet another, pale green and rubbery. They seem to belong to another world, a submarine earth grown dry in the east wind that pales the barks of trees. The countryside is aged and venerable, its expression erased by the searing, whitening wind, like a face that has known the depth of sorrow.

For four days the fields have blanched in the withering air. The land throws up a white light, and the concrete in the yard is whitened in the dry wind, with a black river of ice running across it where someone has emptied a bucket outside the shippon; and in a way that would have been unbelievable a year ago I am glad of its sudden contrast: something for my blurred sight to fasten on.

The cows' footprints in the lane are set in horseshoe ridges. There is no movement in the fields: farm workers are all employed near the yards and buildings, or hedging with a blazing fire of trimmings. Field birds try to get a living, gulls joining their raucous, predatory voices with the plovers' plaintive cries. The small birds do not leave the hedges, but move stiffly among the branches where the few remaining leaves of beech and oak quiver with a parched, husky sound. By the stream frosted grasses bend over water frozen to silence, and rasp at a touch. Dung, carted out over the unyielding ground and dumped in mounds, steaming and black, freezes and pales and at once becomes invisible to me.

The fire in the kitchen licks the logs with whispering tongues while the cats drowse and mutter, and snow, driving on the east wind, shrouds the fields in sleep or death under a leaden sky.

Two days ago Bill Willsworthy died. Very early in the morning, after dozing, his life ebbed away. Today I took Mrs Willsworthy a bunch of snowdrops and yew, the green-white flowers cool among the black-green of the yew. The old man was in his coffin, where his bed had been lately, under the window.

Mrs Willsworthy sat by the fire and talked. She is eighty, she told me; a few months younger than the young man she married fifty-five years ago; and while she talked about him I could hear how she turned to the sheeted coffin, as she had towards his chair when he used to sit by the fire.

She will not be lonely until they take him away. I believe she talks to him continually when they are alone, calling him Father, while he lies, very light in the pool of darkness beneath the lamp on the table, among their collected treasures, and the lamplight makes a moon of the hanging clock-face above the cupboard crammed with Goss china and willow pattern plates.

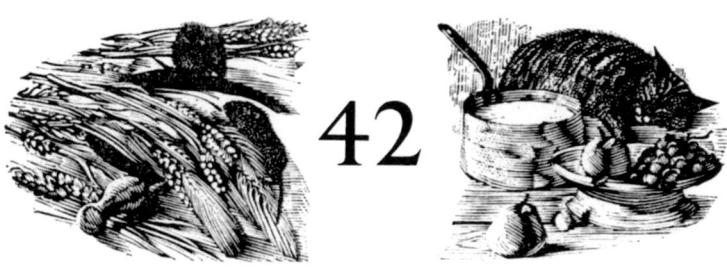

42

Bright sunshine streams across snow, a faultless land-cover fleecing the sounds that fill in my horizon and the echoes shaping it.

In a dazzling world I have to find my way afresh, listening intently, my creaking footsteps disturbing, unseen, the remembered pattern of bird-tracks—the sprays of three delicate points on a stem drawn by the hind claw—ending suddenly where the engraver took to the air, and the places beneath banks churned up by rabbits whose footprints lead despondently into the barren fields. Sometimes a buzzard rises, mewing, from a tree, startling torpid pigeons into flight, and rooks fly up with angry, agitating cries and harry it out of hearing. From their silence I know that hedge birds do not willingly get up, but crouch, sluggish, with feathers bunched. Dick gleefully remembers dogs of the fabulous past catching more rabbits than their masters could carry home, the rabbits losing their bearings in the uniform snow.

A wisp of snipe has come close to the house to dig spear-beaks into the dung-heap, crying 'scape' as they rise in nervous flight. The plover settle at night under a tree in the pasture, changing places with single, wounded cries where the snow will be confused, in the morning, with many footprints so that the grass shows through.

The sun sets on fields in an iron grip, the snow that has melted during the day hanging in icicles from drooping grasses, tinkling at the touch of a boot.

It is only four days since this weather began. And yet—only four days? We are in another existence, in a climate of urgency and constantly boiling kettles, and steaming objects from outside thawing too slowly round the blazing fire: buckets with contents frozen solid, rubber piping blocked by ice, bits of machinery frozen immobile, and garments clotted with frigid snow. The punctual, hackneyed sounds that usually mark the time of day have given way to shouts for hot water, paraffin, methylated spirit, matches, blow-lamps, straw, sacking and help.

Brilliantly sunlit, the freezing days succeed nights when it freezes harder than ever. By day the snow thaws briefly on sunny roofs, dripping dully on to the snow beneath, until the sun sets, and the dripping freezes into silence.

Every morning all the pumps are unworkable, and the tank in the house roof is frozen as well as all the pipes against outside walls. Outside, any metal thing—the handle of a bucket, the lid of a churn—sticks to the hand. Yet my stock geese persist in sleeping in the yard, settling on a sparse patch of dropped hay, facing the wind. Half way through the day, after mooning about grumpily on their former grazing grounds, they come into the yard, ponderous and demanding, and shout for food.

The cows are kept in all day now, and the shippon is warm with their bored and comfortable sighing, which changes, while they eat chopped roots after milking, to a sound like water running into a deep pool: a resonant undertone of heavy breathing and thoughtful chewing, an overtone of crisp biting, the stamp of a hoof, a rattling chain.

The only other warm place out of doors is the barn, where calves are penned in winter; for the calves are separated by a plank partition from the hens on their deep litter of shavings, and the fervour of their busy, cackling life seeps through between the planks on drifts of fine dust that hang on the air like pollen on a summer day. The calves take no notice of the doings next door: the scratching and singing and clucking, the screeches of anger and bustling pursuit and flight. Four or five old hens, broodies who have escaped the pot to raise a family of goslings and survive to rear another, sometimes pause in their foraging on the floor of the barn to consider the goings-on among the captive sisterhood, make some rasping comment, and continue their endless tapping. Outside, on a rippling field of ice and trodden snow, a rush of wings betrays the crowd of small birds who come down to feed with the geese, disturbed, momentarily, by a flurry in the litter house.

Sliding on the pale sky a buzzard calls, outlining its snow-bound hunting ground. Before sunset its crying ceases, and an owl stirs up the starving mice in the frozen rickyard.

43

The cats on the hearth add to their pleasure by stealthy contention for the best place. This morning, after the coldest night, all the pipes were frozen, the pump was frozen, buckets were frozen to the ground, the tractor was frozen, and Dick had to take the churns in a barrow up to the stand in the lane.

We let the cows into the goose field, and Father and Dick drove them down to the stream, which was hacked free of ice at the pool; but the cows kicked up their heels in the sunshine and buried their heads in a pile of old bean straw, capering grotesquely with garlands dangling over one eye, their heavy udders lurching with the exertion of their joyful, ungainly curvetting, and they did not drink. Returning to the shippon half an hour later, they all drank thirstily from their bowls, which cannot be refilled, for the pump that feeds them from the stream is frozen.

After this fruitless exercise Dick came in with the day's supply of logs, illumining his description of the morning's activity with his own special kind of interjection.

' "Help yourselves," I zaid, when us got em down to the stream. "Help yourselves to teddies an' greens. A liddle bit o' meat's ninepence extra." '

If anyone who belongs to this neighbourhood says 'Help yourself,' the offer is almost certain to be followed by an invitation to potatoes and greens. Nancy used to use it; she had it from her mother, and I have heard it from people who came from far beyond our surroundings. We attribute it to some sparing old lady who used to invite visitors to share her dinner on those terms. But when? How long ago? No one seems to know. It belongs with the tales of coincidence that crop up whenever the subject in hand suggests them: tales of deserted loves led by chance to confronting their faithless young men, of nameless sons meeting their fathers, unrecognized.

We like the present to merge with the past. Cicely Rackenford had a girlhood friend who, deserted by her lover, went to a distant village to stay with an aunt, to escape the pity and derision of the neighbours; and on the first Sunday that she was away she heard her false young man's banns called with the name of a girl in that parish. Whenever banns were mentioned when Nancy was here, the story cropped up as though it had all happened yesterday.

Not least of the things that I have lost now that Nancy has gone is my link with the living past, seasoning the present with shrewd jokes, and tales that have the sad inevitability of folk songs. Dick has the fuel, a hoard of memories, but not the tinder of imagination to set it alight, nor her genius for adding chip upon chip of fable and reminiscence to build a little fire.

44

Last night the pipes thawed. It is still freezing, in a fierce white light; but there is some feeling in the air, caught for an instant and lost again, of relaxing tension. The hint is so delicate that it is impossible to tell where it comes from: it is not smelt, nor heard, nor seen. Only after it has made itself apparent, observation supports it. On a high pasture, Dick says, moles have suddenly raised a city of mounds under an oak, profiting by the softening earth; and at the foot of the banks a litter of snail-shells lies at the edge of the lane, scratched out by thrushes and blackbirds from among the dry leaves at the hedge bottom during their desperate search for food: remembered shells of lemon and tortoiseshell and sandalwood colour, and the tabby shells of garden snails, cracking at the touch of a foot. They must have been there for days, but assert their presence only when the weather releases its grasp.

Mr Luppett's ewes are lambing in a field beside the lane, and I leant on the gate, listening to the piping voices of the lambs on the softening air, and the guttural cries of their mothers. One day, this time last year, I met old Bill Willsworthy leaning on the gate where the wet red earth was imprinted with hundreds of sharp, pointed footmarks. The first pair of lambs in the flock had been born, and they stood tottering by their mother's broad side, shaking their donkey ears, switching their tails, the wind carrying away their reedy cries. They nuzzled their dam uncertainly, but she gave them no help. She was absorbed in eating her placenta. Old Willsworthy was slowly recovering from one of his bouts of bronchitis. Wheezing and frail, he refused to go indoors until he had drunk his fill from his own special source of wellbeing.

'When lambs be a little older,' he said, 'they'll collect, about twenty of em, and race and play till they'm exhausted. Then they lay down and get chilled and some'll die. The only thing to stop that is to cut their tails. They won't play no more, then.'

He repeated this bleak little morsel of his experience, then his attention strayed back among his years of lambings in this steep field, perfect for its purpose, where heavy ewes, if they go over on their backs, roll on to their feet again, and newly dropped lambs are safe from swamps. Then he remembered times when he had ploughed it behind horses when it was part of our farm; and while the old man who was still, in his own memory, young, leant on the gate with me, his life flowed past us like a stream, which, while it bubbles into existence on the Moor, at the same time, in full maturity, runs into the sea.

45

In the evening the boys came over to help me with my Braille lesson. The exercises are in the form of a thriller now, and the boys ruthlessly press me to hurry with the preparatory lesson and read the next instalment, urging 'Do brace up, Luce,' as I spell out the tale to them. But my interest leaves theirs far behind, in admiration for the ingenuity of the author who continually repeats the newly learnt symbols in what evolves as a neatly composed whodunit.

The demands of the frost have not spared much time for reading, but it thawed during the night, with rain, and the fields were washed clean this morning. They will be pale, yellowed as though they had been under deep water. There is a feeling of released tension, and in spite of the grip of ice spring has advanced while the land was held. The gander has grown suddenly gallant, walking in advance of his wives, his neck outstretched, hissing.

This morning the familiar sounds of the last fortnight were missing: the tops of churns, frozen on to the neck, being knocked off, and all the sharpened sounds of the fields and the rush of wings as house-fed birds flew up from the yard. Instead, gutters run over and the pastures seethe and water drips off gate-bars and hedges.

When Father came in to breakfast he said the yard looked as though a high tide had receded, leaving behind flotsam of discarded straw left over while he and Dick were lagging pipes, and pieces of sacking which were frozen to the ground and hidden under frozen snow, all lying, now, sodden and untidy. Cans that held paraffin for the blowlamp, rags used for sponging pipes, old churns that were used to carry water —all that was frozen into the landscape lies squalidly now in the slushy yard.

The curious thing is that while we were hurrying about using all our ingenuity to improvise with this rubbish we looked forward longingly to the thaw, and now that it has come at last, we have nothing to meet it with but a grudging demand on listless energy to clear up the deserted field of our miniature battle, remembering almost wistfully the inspiring hardships triumphantly encountered there.

46

A thrush sang in the top of an oak in the high south hedge of the churchyard, and beyond it a thrashing machine worked, loud and clattering, with a 'whish' of sheaves which the men fed to it in silence, out of deference to us, whose customary afternoon had been interrupted because of the Judge's quiet death, four days ago, while he dozed in his chair by the fire. A soft day, such as often follows hard weather, a brooding, pregnant day, its haze palpable with thrashing dust, imminent spring clear in the living smell of the pile of earth at the grave's side, and the thrush's shouted song.

The familiar clatter of the thrashing machine accented the remembered words of the service, and only the unexpected shattered composure. After the blessing, one of the friends whom the Judge used to allude to as though they were a hardly separated family blew 'Gone Away' on the Judge's horn, and hounds instantly answered from the house at the end of the drive, and I believe most of us wept.

Mrs Mowbray, leaning on a stick, said something to each of us as we left, thanking us for coming, telling us, firmly, how thankful she was that he was not the one to be left. 'I expect you noticed that he had grown very deaf.'

Outside the vestry door, on the way home, I met Jim's uncle, the undertaker. He had been paying the bearers, who went home on their bicycles to change the suits that mocked their broad shoulders, before going back to the farms for milking.

Jim's uncle walked down the lane with me, formal in his tail coat, wearing his black gloves, I am sure, and carrying the top hat I have never seen him wear. Old people, he said, mostly die in January or February. You could see that by looking at the headstones in any graveyard. After tea, no doubt, he returned to the work of his building business. It would belittle him merely to say that he carries off the funerals he manages with a flourish, for he has a distinct air, sitting alone in the front pew of the south aisle, with the row of bearers behind him in their tight-backed Sunday suits. Hidden among the flowers on the coffin lies the coil of webbing he will steady it with while the bearers lower it into the grave without bump or hitch.

'I'd like Uncle Perce to bury me,' Nancy used to say. 'He's stylish.'

47

The hens sang this evening in the litter house, a long-drawn note followed by reflective clucking, then the long note again, a sign of satisfaction. Four or five broodies take possession of the nesting box every afternoon, as spring approaches, gathering all the eggs under them, rolling them under with their beaks until all the eggs they can reach are covered by their breast feathers. Then they spread their wings and sit like china birds and shout angrily when the trap door is opened, extending their wings and ruffling out their feathers.

Last year Nancy, shaking a duster out of an upstairs window, discovered a nestful of eggs hopefully concealed by one of the outdoor hens, in a flower bed beside the house.

'There's one above sees all,' she said, and lit the morning with her little joke and the pleasure of the discovery. Now time no longer stands still for a moment while she tells the news in terms that fill the mind with pictures.

'I thought I was sitting my nest lovely,' she would say of a surprise held back from Jim, and add: 'but he were on the laughing side,' on disclosing that he knew about it already.

The year seesaws between winter and spring. For the first time since the end of summer the geese have been down to the water. (They play on the stream at mating time and preen on the banks, standing and stretching their wings with loud clapping.) Hearing them, this evening, was like opening a window and discovering spring, as the gander led his two wives home up the field, exchanging conversation in low, woody voices, as they pitched and rolled over the rutted surface of the meadow.

At every step the pastures fizz and gurgle, still paled by frost and water, but in the soft air birds sing in the hedges: robins and wrens and thrushes, and tits who break off their flinty songs to shake out an angry rattle of warning notes, and treefuls of starlings who sing, in garish unison, a glittering, florid, purring, whistling, beak-smacking song.

Suddenly a curlew called 'Cur-li?' questioning, her voice rising on the last syllable. Once she let fall her bubbling summer cry, and almost at the same moment a lark above the high ploughland sang its close mesh of notes, breaking away from the flock still fluttering, hedge high, with low winter calls.

48

George called at tea-time, finding an excuse to spare himself embarrassment. 'Have you got a piece of string? My bicycle's broken.'

Simon and Peter were already having tea with us, before listening to the current instalment of my Braille thriller. Beyond greeting them, jointly, with a monosyllable, ''lo', George behaved as though they were not there. The companionship of the elder boys seems to have set each of the two adrift in whatever currents of enthusiasm or boredom the other encounters. George is insulated by his own interests, and at that moment he was set on conversation with Father and me.

'It feels like spring, but it's not, yet,' he said; and remembering the hard weather still likely to come he observed, during tea: 'You haven't got many broken windows in this house.'

Father replied: 'I don't think we have. Have you?'

'Yes,' said George; then added, in deference to the family pride, 'What can you expect, with so many people in the house?'

When he had gone home to bed his calves down Simon and Peter settled down to hear my exercise. Urged on by them to spell out the tale as fast as possible I have earned a mild protest from Dr Williams: 'You *are* getting on; but don't be in too great a hurry, will you?'

But there is need for haste; the winter's fitful allowance of personal leisure is almost over. All day a grey wind has rushed through trees, whining round buildings: a north-west wind, lashing vicious strokes of hail and rain. Yet above the roar, down the wind, suddenly came again the curlew's rising cry, bubbling and exultant. In spite of the ravaging day, the year is in ascent.

Yesterday Hetty, the grey goose, laid her first egg. I heard her making her nest in the goosehouse in the morning, gathering straw round her feet with careful movements of her beak, and pictured her face, intent. The gander and his other wife, grey and white Kate, hung about between the stream and the house, calling impatiently, waiting for her until she hurried off to join them at last, after covering her precious egg with straw.

It must be four years since Hetty, who always lays first, at the time of the curlews' return, hurried off, bright-eyed, to join the others after laying her first egg. I thought, then, that it was necessary to replace the eggs that I took to set under broody hens with china ones, and the grey goose was the victim of this unlucky mistake. For a china egg is the size of a hen's egg, and when I took their supper into the goose-house that evening a conversation of some sort had just concluded. Hetty was standing alone in the promising spring twilight, the midget egg exposed. The other two had their heads together.

49

Dying wind all day, until, in the evening, it was still. Half-way down the stream field the gander called stridently for a missing goose. Kate, I believe, was on the stream, silent and watchful, while I climbed the bank on to the little plantation where she laid last year. If she was there she would turn when she saw me, but she did not leave the water.

Under neglected apple trees old grasses lay flattened by storms, the last leaves of the old year scattered over them, crumbling underfoot: leathery oak leaves, lying flat on the ground, crushing dully; beech leaves, curled as they dried, breaking crisp and shrill, disturbing the quiet that was never so potent as now, in the haze of half-seeing.

There is an air of secrecy about the place. A pair of long-tailed tits came to the hedge leaning over the stream, calling with their thin bell-notes, leaving one sapling for another in looping, whispering flight. Once Father started making this place into a nursery for little apple trees, but then—perhaps old age suddenly caught up with him—it was forgotten, and its air of solitude depends on its being uncultivated, while even the wind cannot reach it to sweep away one year's decay before another's growth succeeds it.

Caught everywhere by trailing dog rose, and brambles that crawl among the bent grass and loop trailers among the branches of apple trees and sprawl over them in shapes of awnings and arches, I struggled over the plot feeling under tents of last year's skeleton flowers. Kate had been there. I felt the place where her last year's nest was made: it had been scooped clear of leaves. I am sure that if I could have seen them here and there white feathers rested on the sodden earth, feathers delicately curled, and that she watched me as she lurked on the water.

As I left the plantation the gander continued to call. On neighbouring farms one would turn to another over tea, hearing him calling, and say: 'Someone have a goose laying out.'

The place is an island in all but the driest weather, a pear-shaped half acre with the stream shaping its rounded end and a rivulet dividing at the point and flowing down each side to join the main stream. Oak and ash and beech and elm border the runnels, the wind rushing through their heads. On the main stream the geese lead a secret life, paddling silently round the bend, dipping their necks to pass under low branches of sallow and elder, sliding out of sight.

Last year, after many days of searching, I found Kate in this place, brooding nine eggs. As I came near she lowered her head on her breast in a sweet and vulnerable attitude, maternal and feminine, until I walked close, thinking she had just laid, when she stood and exposed the eggs, brown and tawdry from her muddy feet, stretching her neck and hissing savagely, with extended wings. I left her, and the knowledge of her secret vigilance pervaded the spring, making it more vivid, as though I should have guessed that I should not see another.

Four weeks of my last seen spring focused on this place because Kate brooded her eggs in the nest above the stream. Brambles and old grasses protected her, cushions of primroses covered the banks. Wrens moused in and out of the brushwood in the hedge bottoms surrounding her; all the birds of spring quarrelled and sang and flighted above her. One sunny day, while she sat, a cuckoo called for the first time; she paid no more attention to it than she did to the silent gulls who flew over in rough weather, leisurely and reserved as fish.

In the early morning I used to sit on a bank of the island, going out of my way to fetch vegetables from the garden. Every blade of the pasture shone in the sun, with small flies dancing an endless measure above them. Bird-shadows passed over the grass and a curlew would alight on the pasture, ashen grey against the half-bare hedges, with a momentary flash of cream as it lifted its wings and showed its breast on landing. A warbler would sing a short phrase in one of the trees on the bank, a moorhen croaked below me, but the wind made no sound in the trees whose leaves, of perfect adult form, almost impudent in imitation, were no bigger than a little fingernail.

Sometimes in the evening I would sit there again after driving the cows to a far pasture, trees bending over me, and in their shade flies dancing over the water, parting and meeting, silently breaking the surface and leaving a ring that widened in multiplying circles until the last one disappeared. Primroses and violets grew on long stems in a bed of dried and tangled grass and sere leaves. On the lush south bank stitchwort and ragged robin overtopped the fading flowers of early spring. Once, overnight, speedwell showered the banks in pools of deep blue. The blue sky still hung in the meshes of the oaks' knotted twigs and the elms' angled branches, but looking up under a beech the very light was green, filtered through fragile, transparent leaves edged and covered with down.

Day by day the white and grey goose sat, silent and watchful, in air too still to disturb the unblown dandelion clocks, while the first butterflies hovered and dipped above flowering grasses drooping under their light burden of lemon- and lavender- and rust-coloured flowers. I never saw her stealthy departure from the nest, nor her return after bathing and feeding; the only movement she ever allowed me to see was her industrious replenishment of the sides of the nest with twigs she reached for with serpentining neck. The only sign I had that the brood was hatching was an empty shell behind her one day, turned out of the nest.

Kate hatched six goslings. On the following morning they

sat beside her on the beautiful nest of down and feathers, crowding against her side, pure primrose colour. I took them some bread and milk, and she menaced me with wings outspread. The air was filled with the scent of water mint crushed as I crossed the little ford; the steep banks of the plantation were still lined with primroses and violets, and apple blossom bent over the nest. In the afternoon she tipped her family out of this little paradise, and I saw them swimming with her on the stream, bobbing in a close flotilla. They could never return to their nest above the steep bank.

In the evening Kate took her goslings from the stream up the long, steep meadow to the goosehouse to join the gander and the other goose. The newly hatched chicks must have had a hard journey, clambering in and out of deep cowfootprints, weaving through the rushy grass up the steep hill, falling into ruts baked hard in the sunshine, the sun beating on their pollen down.

Outside the goosehouse Kate kept her young by her feet. When I scattered bread soaked in milk for them she offered it to the gander, and when he had had his fill she finished it, motioning the goslings back with her beak. She drank from the bowl of water I put down, but ordered the goslings away. When they played at snatching blades of grass from among the few weeds growing in the caked earth the other goose pushed them away, and the mother, with an infinitely protective movement of her head, held close over the huddled group, bade them be still.

I left them in the goosehouse, for when I tried to intervene, the goslings were in danger of being trodden on while the two geese and the gander attacked me, and there they spent the night. All the next morning Kate kept her family in the house, where she and the gander waited for Hetty, who was laying an egg, until, as the goslings had had no water since the day before, I took them away in a basket after a battle with the gander, who flew at my face with beating wings. I should not have been able to gather them up if an inquisitive heifer had not put her nose round the door to find out what the clatter was about, and distracted the gander's attention.

I put them with a hen who had just hatched three goslings, in a coop in the orchard.

All the geese were in a frenzy, and Kate stormed across the yard into the pasture, where I saw her standing and calling, searching the distance with neck upstretched, when I went in to dinner. The little goslings gratefully crept under the nurse hen.

The stillness followed that falls in the dinner-hour on a farm—quiet broken only by a stray hen knocking over a bucket, or momentary bickering among the pigs, then the silence settles again. Shadows lie black and still in the yard. A butterfly flutters over to settle on the warm stone of a wall.

After dinner I went to look over the hedge at the geese. Kate was standing among them. Close round her feet her goslings clustered. In silence she had been to the orchard and collected her own family, leaving their three companions with the nurse hen. She had crossed the yard and walked up the gritty lane, then into the goose field with her tired little family. Still she would not let them eat. With a gentle, imperious gesture, stretching her head over them, she kept them round her feet on the hot, baked, trodden earth outside the goosehouse, while the other geese grazed.

There was no trace of struggle by the coop in the orchard. The hen was sitting on the three young she had raised, looking faintly put-out.

I went back to the kitchen and fussed. 'Kate would defend those goslings with her life, but she's going to let them starve and die of thirst.'

Father looked over his spectacles, above the local paper. 'D'you think they had any grub while they were with the hen?'

'I simply don't know what happened . . .'

'If I were you I shouldn't worry.' He returned to the paper drowsily. 'Children soon learn to manage their parents.'

 # 50

I never remember which is the calendar's first day of spring; but every year one day comes, when, although there is no obvious change in the appearance of trees and hedges, the earth seems to breathe, and it is spring. Then, in the old days, I used to discover that very small nettles were pushing through holes in a broken bucket in the bottom of a hedge; and earth turned over with a finger exhaled a living smell; and hazel catkins, until then apparently carved from wood, were gosling green beneath the smoky scales, and catkins of pussy willow shone white in the sun. Once, as a child, I pulled one of those to pieces, determined to find the source of the rose tint beneath the silver fur, and discovered the bright rose-coloured scales covering the little body under the down.

The days that follow often bring winter back with cold intensified by a day's unkept promise, delaying its going with soft-falling feathers of snow which new grass pricks, when it thaws, with multitudes of holes. But, when the curlews come, and the geese start laying, spring begins for me, though the plover, still flocking, may flicker and turn against winter-dark woods.

Now is the time when I set the first broody hen on four goose eggs in a coop in the ramshackle shed in the orchard, where nurse-hens bring off the first goslings every year. The shed is really a hovel, an eyesore of buckled strips of galvanized iron roofing a half-rotten structure of dilapidated wooden walls, too decayed to house any creature with more strength to destroy it than a hen, too broken-down for use as a store, yet invaluable as cover for hens each brooding a clutch of four eggs. All but the most model farms seem to conceal some such shanty, treasured by the farmwife, and essential to her private economy.

Kate has changed her mind about laying in the plantation this year, and has built a nest in the heifers' house, a three-sided shed attached to the goosehouse where Hetty lays; and the gander, very conveniently for him, can sit on the grass in front of the partition between the sheds, at an equal distance between his two wives, while he waits, with easily shattered patience, for them to come out.

A goose egg fills the hand, rough to the touch. I do not think I ever noticed this before; but now the weight of it, the curve of it in the palm, is more telling than sight, as evocative as the dust-laden shafts of sunshine slanting through the crumbling slats in the side of the shed, and the dry smell of old wood and the warm, earthy floor, and the hot, pricking smell of nettles that grow through where the rotten boards of the wall meet the ground.

Now the feel of a thing brings all its dimensions and its secret peculiarities immediately before my inward eye. Richard, who taught me that, learnt it from his father, who picked it up watching medical students anxiously fingering bones before examinations, memorizing every feature of ridge and depression, of rough surface and smooth, reconstructing, by memory, the complexity of the moving structure depending on their framework.

Very many times I have watched my broodies feeding and returning to the nest, and now the impress of an egg in my hand brings back to sight the exquisite delicacy of a hen arranging her bulky weight on a fragile clutch of eggs. I know how she would stand, alert on one foot, with the other held beneath her, the claws relaxed and folded, peering left and right with extended neck and sharp jerking of her head, slanting her aquiline gaze to look with one eye at the eggs, until, stepping forward to one side of the nest, she plants her feet dextrously among them.

When a hen is broody she abandons her darting, cackling habit, and becomes gentle and decorous in voice and manner; and while she turns to face the front of the nest as she slides her feet over and among the eggs, she discovers the balance and composure of a rather ponderous tightrope-walker, until she settles down, rocking as she arranges her legs among her brood, bending her head from side to side to push under her any egg that is showing. Then, lifting her chest, she drops her breast-feathers over the eggs in front of her, sinking her head among the feathers of her neck, in the position she will not change until the front of the coop is removed for her to come out and feed in the morning.

I find that I am growing noisy, to fill the place of things unseen, perhaps; for the thoughts of solitary workers drift on a meandering stream whose course winds in and out among visible surroundings.

I was first aware of this while I was making butter; though the earliest stage of butter-making, as I was taught by my mother, cannot but be almost silent while the brittle crusts of scalded cream are turned in a basin with hands washed first in hot water, then in cold, to prevent it from sticking. Kneading the crumbling mass until it changed its texture, beginning to bind, massing into pale butter with thick buttermilk running out, I found that soon the cheerful sound of the basin rocking on the table quickened my thoughts, and tags of my mother's old advice came back to mind.

'Butter making softens the nails.' Her hands were pink and satiny after making butter, but the nails were always short on the right hand since her young womanhood, when she used to make ten or twelve pounds every week for market.

''Tis the quality of the water makes the butter.' In days which seem, in retrospect, as though they must have contained more hours, Mother used to walk to a distant spring for clear, cold water.

I poured cold water from the tap over the knob I had made, kneading it under water, growing, I suppose, more and more noisy, splashing, and bumping the basin in the sink, washing away the buttermilk; for, when I had salted it and began shaping it on the table with the patters, one of the cats sprang from the fireside on to the back of a chair to see what was going on, and Father, who had just come in, observed mildly: 'You make a noise like an old-fashioned grocery shop.'

I wonder whether I make a busy noise to smother my fears, for the onrush of spring, with its sudden recurrences, is a continual reminder that my mind is full of pictures that have no chance of renewal; it is an album of fading views.

When I had finished making butter I went out and sat on a bank in the sunshine. The wind on the other side of the hedge rushed over a field, ebbing and flowing where there were no trees to catch and resist it, with the sound of heavy breathing; and I thought I would not grope after an unseen spring, only lie and listen in the warm, pricking sunshine that raised the scent of nettles, hot and heavy.

A lark spun its song high in the sky, somewhere a buzzard called and was answered, a chaffinch which had staked a claim in the hedge called 'pink, pink, pink', and shouted a jaunty song finishing with the brusque enquiry: 'What's it now?' In the water-meadows a curlew rose with a rippling song that ceased the moment it alighted.

Everyone was ploughing, harrowing, or spreading manure, with humming tractors moving slowly over the fields, pursued by flocks of gulls which made no sea cries, but vented dry, rapacious sounds as they flung themselves on to the newly turned furrows. It was impossible to shut out the memory of them swirling into the air like paper-ash as the tractor and plough returned, and circling and plunging to earth again; and their noisy foraging brought to mind one of spring's earliest, best loved harbingers: the purple bloom on the tops of elms bordering red land which paled, as harrowed earth dried, in close lines like a head of well-combed hair.

I suppose it is from a collection of such indestructible snap-shots that I shall find, when the time comes, material to babble, like old Falstaff, of green fields.

52

I have finished the Braille course. For the last time the boys have read Dr Williams's letter to me in schoolmasterly voices, looking for praise they might take credit for, pleased that she complimented me on the Braille books that I sent back to her, for sometimes, it seems, the anxious fingers of beginners press the dots flat. Now she warns me not to hurry to read heavy stuff, and I shall cut my teeth on *The Scarlet Pimpernel*, transcribed by her in the simplest form.

I shall miss the companionship of the discerning mind that worked out the lessons so that they never seemed over-hard. Once one of the boys asked: 'What's it like, learning to read up your arm?' It is a path where concentration leads to peaks of triumph, and untried senses discover new prospects of visualization.

In the evening I went to tell Mrs Mowbray that I have finished.

Facing the empty chair by the hearth, she maintains alone the defiance of old age she used to share with the Judge, and has diverted her critical sallies, once parried by her yoke-fellow with disarming blandness, towards Mr Silvester.

'What does he say, Lucy? Silvester, you've left your teeth out again. No one can hear a word you say.'

Mr Silvester, who had shouted to ask whether he might remove the tea things, unable to hear her reply, returned a mildly sarcastic condolence on her deafness. Neither has any real heart for the game; and even the cat, lapping mincingly from the jug, and disturbed with an angry flurry when the tray was moved, seemed to be playing a part that was expected of it.

I have a feeling that they are all copying a pattern they once traced spontaneously with variations inspired by the moment. Only when we were alone the obstinate old lady relaxed with an unsuppressed sigh of relief, metaphorically putting her feet up until such time as her contemporary's re-entry should jerk her into setting him an example again.

While we were alone she gave me a Braille watch that she had asked a friend to buy. It turned out to be a man's pocket watch, since she had not specified whom it was for; but that does not matter, for I shall keep it indoors to use as a clock.

I have never worn a wrist-watch out of doors. Like other people who live mostly in the open air I can guess the time, not so much by actively studying the position of the sun, which is far from visible all the year round, as by a series of appraisals that have become instantaneous in a lifetime of use, and so deep-rooted in habit that it is almost impossible to sort them into single file: a glance at the sky to discover I hardly know what, a change of light, perhaps, while the eye, without bidding, takes in the earth's response to the light. At the same time other perceptions slide back to the last moment when time was fixed—probably a meal, unfailingly punctual—and forward to try to find how far away the next demand—probably another meal—seems to be. A background of customary sounds plays some part: a flight of homing birds, the rattle of a bucket, the protests of hungry poultry or calves, children playing their way to and from school. One's ear trains itself.

It is only possible for people whose life follows the same path every day, but still there must be many like me who can guess what time it is to within a few minutes any day out in the fields. An element of guesswork comes in, and one has to launch oneself on one's decision; certainly it is disastrous to start analysing and doubting—second thoughts invariably turn out to be wrong. Perhaps some unrecognized sense comes into use.

On the following morning I took the Braille watch in my pocket when I went out, I do not really know why. Possibly to test its efficiency beside my other way of deciding the time. Flat and smooth in the hand, it is cased on both sides, the face exposed by pressing the winder; a glassless face, marked with a raised dot at each hour, and double dots at the quarters. Feeling with the forefinger it is not difficult to find the point of the hour hand, short of the dots, and the minute hand reaching over them, an action which could become as perfunctory as a glance at a clock, if fingering were as quick as sight. But waiting brings an expansion of sense, a kind of listening, only more complex. It is as though one threw out feelers.

Searching the face of the watch, it seemed as though the sky grew higher and the horizon moved away. I have no idea whether I stood there for a long time, or for a short time that seemed long. The time filled the horizon and the dome of the sky.

 ## 53

Owls call now in the hazy afternoon, and curlews get up in the night and join their voices with the plovers' lost cries. Small birds, distracted by the fury of mating, fly hedge-high in flight and pursuit and brush past one's ear, indifferent to human presence.

There is a common belief that when sight diminishes hearing is intensified—an observation made, I would say, by onlookers. I doubt whether I hear more acutely than before, but every trifle heard passes under expert scrutiny in some formerly idle workshop in my mind, and hearing seems to be intensified.

In the last exercise of Dr Williams's course there was a poem by William Blake, *The Echoing Green*, a little song of pleasure in the springtime games of village children. Its title, as a refrain, slid into the minor key with evening and the end of play as 'the darkening Green'; and the variation, with its undertone of regret, brought me face to face with a change that has stolen into my response to impressions. The thronging animation implied in the first refrain is a challenge which I meet shrinkingly, and the sober modification is a reassurance. For whereas I once felt my way in the dark like everyone else who can see, now undemanding darkness is my ally, and I have to feel my way in the light; nevertheless in daylight new devices sometimes lead me to unexpected rewards.

I begin to recognize likenesses in the voices of people whose difference of outlook and behaviour makes the similarity laughable. Sometimes I wonder whether, if I should see clearly again, I should find appearances a hindrance to perception. When mothers say, of one of their children, 'He's like his dad,' often for me all likeness is missing, and another of the family, possibly the image of his mother, is fixed, by some inflexion of speech, as his father's double. Now even the sound of a footfall reveals a familiar face. A phrase of sound, in its accustomed place, constructs a scene.

As the geese came down to the stream early this morning I was ahead of them, on the opposite bank, on my way home from taking the cows out after milking. They came down the rough field with ponderous care, their everyday pleasantries punctuating their floundering progress, and this is what I saw.

Reaching the brink they launched themselves and slid away on the water, their orange feet paddling leisurely behind, fishing, burying their heads and searching the mud.

When they had exhausted their pleasure in rediscovering the stream they began to wash, dipping breasts and necks and heads into the water and rising to throw it over them, their plumage glowing like pearl. They repeated this over and over again in sheer joy, then one by one they climbed on to the shallow beach. There they smoothed their breast feathers, brushing the water off, then with serpentine writhing of their necks they rolled their heads and the underside of their beaks on the oil-gland above their tails and began a minute grooming, combing the long quills of their wings, gripping each in a beak that slid down its length, returning to the oil-gland and polishing backs and wings with the side of their heads. Twisting, coiling, they polished breasts and stomachs, combing between their feathers, shifting their weight from foot to foot with clownish awkwardness in startling opposition to the elastic grace of their necks, straddling to stretch their wings.

Save for the snapping of their beaks and the clatter of wings they were silent from the moment they left the water, and I, the better to see, had closed my eyes. When I opened them the geese had gone. Noiselessly they had taken to the water and slipped round the bend in the stream under the pendant hazel catkins to play and fish and make love.

54

The time of sales has come round again—of farms changing hands at Lady Day—and I cannot help wondering how long it will be before our farm is one of the spring or autumn meeting places of old farmers—growing fewer every year—wearing celluloid collars with a stud in front, who talk about their neighbours, and the young gentlemen in cord trousers and duffle coats, discussing milk yields and pedigrees. I try not to spoil the occasion with misgivings about the uncertainty of our future, and the young men add to my self-persuaded illusion of permanence with their repetition of well-known half-joking requests for Father's advice, which he answers in the vein they expect: 'Get as near the Show Ring as you like, but never go in.'

In the farmhouses, where wives of the old sort, in voices like the surge and fall of a placid tide, gossip about their families, the weather, and their opinion of the sale—'all the liddle nestle-tripes put together to make a litter'—the stream of conversation is fed by a new spring.

'Darling. Are we going to meet at dinner tonight? Good, then we shan't feel quite so awful about being late. I simply can't think why anyone asks us now they know we're never on time. But however early we milk we're certain to be chasing up stray heifers or something when we should be dressing.'

As we drift through the crowded rooms the voice is

drowned in a pool of local news, then reappears in the main stream, grumbling unregretfully.

'Stephen used to be quite a considerate husband when he was a city gent. But the day we moved in he coolly demanded supper for five men at about half-past nine, and he's gone on like that ever since.'

Another voice condoles and is submerged.

A few years ago talk like that was rare enough to add no more than a trickle to the flood of neighbourly chatter. Now it is an acknowledged tributary. Hardly a farm has been sold in the district recently but has gone to a gentleman farmer— of the new kind, a working man, now, if ever there was one. Their experience, for the most part, is book-learning, and their capital—by the time they have paid for stock and their equipment—probably little more than their physical strength and determination. Their wives, who have not joined us because they were particularly discontented with a previous way of life, but because their husbands find this one more to their liking, in spite of unaccustomed and often gruelling hard work still maintain a semblance of their former social life, with a kind of dedicated frivolity wholly admirable in the face of the obstacles they have to overcome.

Somewhere in the room I hear Pamela. She will be looking, almost certainly, as though she had come to sell clothes pegs —rebellious equally against dining out and all its implications and the conventional observances of traditional farmwives. 'Have the kids told you we're getting an electricity plant?'

Such affluence is unheard of in that house, which would not be itself without chaos of shouting and upbraiding at dusk, when none of the oil-lamps can be found in darkness, and when discovered are empty of oil, and when refilled must still wait for lighting until someone finds matches. It seems that George's godfather, who always sends the children a handsome present at Christmas and Easter, has offered to pay for a plant so that they shall have light for their homework.

'You'll have lights in the shippon first, and a milking

machine,' someone says, and catching sight of old friends who sold their farm at Michaelmas, remarks how smart they look now, adding with mock envy, 'So could we all, I suppose, if we sold up.'

'We should very soon be threadbare,' says Mrs Shenley.

What an odd lot we are, utterly diverse, yet each submitting to something that binds us willingly to the land; to the urgencies and hardships and demands that keep us from what other people call pleasures, for the uncertain reward of harvests laboriously won; obeying a subtle bidding of the kind that calls men to the sea.

 **55**

Not every year does the weather fulfil the mood of the day. Good Friday has been a day of tremulous light, of pale, clear sky and naked trees and an ashen road to church. A day of mocking loveliness.

Easter Day, veiled, and the air warm and syrupy, is from a different climate, the silver light gone with the north-west wind that brought it, and the earth at once more lush, the church filled with the delicate, mossy scent of primroses and the vivid, earthy smell of moss.

The nights continue the mood of days of high wind and driving showers. Curlews get up and cry in a fitful, rain-laden wind; with no knowledge of how the day had gone one might guess, from the birds' wakefulness, that it is a night of pale stars and ragged clouds racing across the moon. The curlews' call, wild and piercing, translates into sound the teeming cloud and moonlight.

The first goslings, pecking and piping in the eggs, tap and scrape while they work to break the shell and tear open the parchment skins enfolding them, while the hen sits, with feathers outspread, croaking occasionally in a voice that has discovered some semblance of the purring note of a mother cat or a cow bending her broad face over her calf; and the complicity of sound and memory reveals the fecund countryside: the ploughland flushed with the green upsurge of spring corn; the trees' pregnant outlines thickened with buds pressed against the sky; pairing buzzards, coloured like moths, on still, spread wings, sliding in and out of an aerial circle in the flirtation of mating; sulphur-yellow butterflies meandering down banks and hedges, suddenly rising and gone in amorous chase.

The hen will not leave the nest until the eggs have hatched, though she makes no objection to their being taken out for the inspection I gave them once, but have to exchange now for listening, holding them hot and vibrant against my ear.

No longer able to meet the expectant eye beneath the hole,

hardly bigger than a match-head, that the most forward chick will have made in some twenty-four hours of working, nor to watch the writhing, convulsive fight of the imprisoned bird, I can still feel the strong, outward thrust of the shell which in contention with such infant strength must be as hard as concrete; and this struggle between birth and death has lost none of its shared intensity. It is as though the hand of Providence lifted, and the choice between oblivion and survival rested with the bird.

I used to take over and carefully pick away small pieces of shell, and moisten the leathery skins beneath, one enclosing the folded body, the other lining the shell. A goose broods her eggs beneath down moist and steamy after swimming in the stream, and keeps the lining pliable, but the eggs under a hen grow dry even though they are sprinkled with water every time she comes off to feed.

Picking away the shell is sure-fingered work, for it is attached by the inner skin to the back of the chick, and clumsiness or haste would result in the gosling's bleeding to death. Disasters like that compose the small-talk of farmers' wives in the hatching days of spring, and once I used to act on a limitless wealth of blood-curdling advice tempered with sober experience. Now I dare not attempt it. I can only wait until the first little bird emerges—waiting is the bane of diminished sight: waiting for help, for lost things to be found, for events to take their course—then I can still forestall one of the many hazards that attend this trifling battle for life by removing the chick so that the remaining eggs shall not crush it, and the empty shell also. For once, when a clutch of eggs was hatching, the half shell of a bird that had emerged fixed itself over the shell of one not yet hatched, fitting over the hole it had diligently pecked, and at the moment of attaining freedom the bird still in the egg was suffocated.

Nature is rich and lavish and careless, and the art of farming is in making the most of its affluence while out-manoeuvring the spendthrift destruction that makes room for survivors. Fledgelings tipped out of overcrowded nests, a rabbit's pitiable remains where a hawk has made a dinner, the multitudinous deaths by flood and storm and drought, accident and the cunning of the hunter, all compensate for spring's boisterous fertility. Farmers, grudging pupils of Nature (whom most of them would like to teach a lesson or two), have a riddle that tersely exemplifies the drain, by over-stocking, on limited keep: 'What is a sheep's worst enemy?' 'Another sheep.'

The newly hatched gosling came back to the house tucked into my coat, and settled down in a flannel-covered box, where it dried into a pancake of catkin-coloured fluff which even my blurred sight distinguishes from the yellow down of a bird that will one day be white. Goslings that will grow into grey geese are clothed in a colour that is a mixture, with changing depths, of yellow and green and grey.

When Moses Primrose went to the fair where he exchanged his father's colt for a gross of green spectacles he wore a waistcoat of 'gosling green'. It is the almost indescribable colour of a willow catkin with the addition of yellow to its grey down. A man of less keen perception than the Vicar of Wakefield might have described the waistcoat as orchid green. It is possible that he wished to give a hint of the goose in his son: the goose-character that emerges from the shell, frank and friendly, that answers with cheerful whistles when spoken to, and continues confiding and gullible until it finds its way on to the table at Michaelmas or Christmas as a roast.

Every year, while I help the goslings out of their shells, Moses Primrose comes into mind while I kneel on the dry, earthy floor of the shed, with his 'green paltry spectacles'.

57

The four goslings squat round a shallow bowl of water, and converse, with the gestures of adult geese. I can still remember, by the prompting of their voices, how they flop in a circle as one starts a conversation which passes round the ring in a crescendo of excited piping and dies down to be renewed, after momentary silence, by another member of the family. It is not the sound of argument, but of eager, unanimous accord, and will continue throughout their lives whenever they come across a pan of water, or a convenient puddle.

From time to time they will toddle a few steps and pretend to pluck grasses, or shovel with their beaks in a plate of bread and milk, then they turn to the water and bury their heads in it, throwing bright drops over their backs, and on uncertain legs perform a sketchy pantomime of grooming until, tired, they obey the clucking of their hen mother, and I know by their silence when they have crept under her broad wings and the curtain of her breast feathers.

At night, before I close the coop which stands in the orchard now, I speak to them, kneeling on the grass, and heads immediately appear above the mother's wings and beneath her breast, answering excitedly, the more assertive ones stumbling forward, gabbling enthusiastic replies.

In a thundery spring they have a lawn of a few turves in front of the coops in the shed, so that they may play at grazing, safe from the weather, for after their first day they need grass to crop. Once, when I was away during a thunderstorm I found the hen mother of five goslings sitting, placid and drenched, in the orchard when I returned. In a stricken semicircle before her all but one of her family sprawled, colourless, sodden, and dead. The heavy rain falling on their backs had killed them as they ran towards her. Only the one beneath her was alive; it also was drenched, but had not had the shock of rain falling on its back. When I had put it in a basket by the fire I picked up the hen and shook her for her carelessness. It relieved my feelings and caused her very little inconvenience.

Yet what could she have done? If she had fussed about the birds that were already dead she might have lost the one survivor. Maternal animals follow the pattern of their kind: the hen would have called and squatted when the rain began, and when one chick crept under her her purpose was fulfilled. Usually the majority obey a call and the plan works out satisfactorily. I have watched, with dismay that seems to be characteristic only of the human mind, one chick stranded and calling in vain while a moorhen floated away with the rest of her brood washed out of the nest in a flood.

Every farmer knows what happens to the weakling in a litter of pigs: it remains the nestle-tripe. If animals make a favourite of one of their young it is almost always the best specimen, and I wish I might imitate my companions' flat refusal to cry over spilt milk.

58

While the goslings follow their busy mother over the orchard grass the swift beat of wings and sudden silence, as nesting birds disappear into hedges or under the eaves of the house or between the gaping planks of a shed, punctuate the slow defile of spring days. Spring comes haltingly to land which confronts the Moor; bitter air keeps the days cool and the nights silver. In the early morning drifts of blackthorn flowers lean over white, frosted meadows where, as sunshine melts the rime on the open fields, trees still cast white shadows. On such days the advance of the season is arrested in the searching, frosty sunshine.

In sheltered places butterflies will settle, flat and still, on red banks where rabbits have made a fine tilth among bright beds of nettles. Above them enamelled and goffered holly leaves shine in the sun, wine-coloured brambles bear small perfect leaves edged with dark red, elder bushes carry grey-green leaves, and small leaves glisten on the thorn. But in the bud ash leaves will lie clasped, one above the other, pressing to burst their black cases, until, freed, they will still bend over one another, the small leaves folded with the ribs pressed close together along the spine, like sculptured feathers.

Robins build in rabbit-scratches on the banks: nests of moss behind a parted curtain of drooping grasses. To my intent ear it seems that birds hurry all day on crowded thoroughfares with material for their building: a strand of cow-hair, a feather caught as it drifted in the air, a tuft of rabbit-down snatched from some scene of murder in the fields.

Or there are days of 'growing weather', the sky all grey, diminishing from violet to white. Then, instead of the stiff breeze, light airs carry the curlews' call and the cry of plover. Trees, instead of enmeshing the sun's light, stand sombrely in the pastures; and in the heavy, moist air it is hardly fanciful to imagine the sound of sap rising, until it is forgotten in hours of cold rain, with bitting, unabating wind which persists when the rain ceases and the sun shines.

Yet, one day, in the meadow where the heifers graze, where the wind does not penetrate, a cuckoo will call, and in spite of the black weather green will spring in the hedges, and where there was only a bloom on red fields suddenly there will be a cover of level green, and while ash trees still wait to burst their buds, beeches will disclose a lovely cinnamon sheen, raising slender buds from level branches on twigs spread like the fingers of an upturned hand.

Dick came, this morning, to set mole traps in my garden, gossiping while he dug his knotty fingers into the fine tilth of the molehills toppling the seedlings, where, spring after spring, moles hunt and gorge in the worm-stocked, extravagantly manured earth.

'See the Indian gentleman, time ago, come selling ties? Wanted to sell me one, but I tol' un I got one. "You got a lucky face," er says. "I've heard that afore," I zaid. Then 'e puts 'is hand inside 'is coat, see,'—from the altered direction of his voice I could tell that Dick leant back on his heels to demonstrate—'an' drops something into mine. 'Twas a bead. "Keep this," er says, "an' you'll have jolly good luck." '

Dick put the bead in my hand. He had tied it to a piece of string.

'I wanted to keep un safe,' he explained. 'I thought: I'll keep ee, maister, an' see what you do do. "I'll be back in six months," the Indian zaid, "an' before that you'm going to have some jolly good luck." Yes, I thought, you come back, mate, an' I ain't had none. But it's begun to work. I picked up a halfpenny the other day. That's the start, I reckon. Don't want nothing flashy to once. Get another bead nex' time er comes, an' see if I don' make a penny.'

Half joking, half believing in his talisman, with the sun resting on the back of his faded jacket, he was as clear in my mind's eye, from years of repetition of the job he was doing, as the climate of the day: the dome of the sky clear blue to the paling horizon, the Moor a shape of blue against it, a blue and milky light resting on red fields rolled after sowing with grass, and in the rich air a cuckoo's voice, mellow and veiled. Only the ash spears in the hedges enclosing the garden, polished and olive-coloured, carry hard, soot-coloured buds, which I can feel between finger and thumb, undisturbed by the sunshine; and they have some affinity with the cautious, hardy old figure in its weathered casing that stooped over the warming earth of the seed bed.

I could tell from his attitude that he was hollowing out a molehill, from either side of which a tunnel would run: the mole's road; and across the path he would set his first trap, an ancient, scissor-like instrument with a collar arranged to spring the scissors on the mole's poor little body if it should put its head through. Unlike Dick, whose person, clothes and belongings have a quality of age so ingrained that they are dateless, his mole traps evoke an era: they are medieval in conception, as uncompromisingly functional as old instruments of torture.

He stood up stiffly, to stretch his heron legs, and I guessed that he had finished with the first run. He would have covered the basin with dock leaves sprinkled with mud to keep out the light.

'That'll fix un,' he said, and added his yearly conclusion: 'Moles do go along at eight, twelve, and four o'clock, feeding,' and he turned to the sun in a business-like way, as a guard, before signalling a train, looks at his watch.

The first time he set his traps in my garden I went to look at them after each of his appointed hours, in case a mole had been caught and not killed. They had not caught anything. They never have. But every year Dick fixes the moles with his traps; for disturbed on their pleasure ground they go away.

Dick bent to another run while I prepared a nursery for the young leeks I shall transplant when he has sent the moles packing. Sometimes a female cuckoo raised her voice in bubbling excitement, with a cry like water running out of a bottle. A thrush sang from the top of a tree, wrens and warblers in hedges, tits in the orchard, robins on walls, and on an outstretched twig of the garden hedge a chaffinch shouted angrily 'Whit-ting-ting,' until, mollified by the sunshine, he found himself singing, ending each phrase with the enquiry 'What's for dinner?'

Dick finished his second trap. 'Good thing Nance don't know us've set these,' he said with satisfaction. 'Er wouldn't like it.'

'If that was the only kind of teasing Nancy got she wouldn't have had much to complain of,' I said.

Dick added a few careful touches to his work. 'Us didn't terrify Nance more'n was good for her,' he said decidedly.

'Why did you torment her at all?'

For years we have retreated from this argument at this point, after discovering the futility of trying to meet in a thicket of prejudiced reasoning. But in the bird-filled sunshine it seemed possible, just for once, that we might find our way to a clearing in the dark wood; and Dick, for a wonder, relaxed his sentinel habit of silence.

'I like Nance, an' I wouldn't do nothing unkind to her, but she'm different,' he said conclusively.

The only way to keep such talk conversational is to go slowly, otherwise it hurries down a dead-end. At the bottom of a hedge a willow warbler was building. Dick broke off to tell me what she was about, and I know her well, for she has built in other years, and while I worked she would bring lengths of reed, flying to an old half-uncoiled roll of wire netting, perching on its edge to glance sharply round, disappearing among the nettles and grasses under the hedge.

She is coloured like spring, a mixture of green and brown and grey, so that no one could say what colour she is: the colour of trees newly fledged, and fields where green mists the earth. I never looked for her nest. I hardly dared to pause by the wire when I used to walk round the garden. If I stopped working she stopped building. Sometimes when I looked up from hoeing she would be there, on the wire, more often she was not. Yet, as I stooped over the earth I knew that she came and went, silent and absorbed.

There is nothing of the naturalist in Dick, who treats all

creatures, wild and domesticated, not as equals, but as having the same intelligence as he; teasing them as he might good-naturedly tease a child: withholding the cows' food momentarily to laugh at their expression of anxious indignation, hiding the kittens from the mother cats. So, while he described with affectionate detail the movements of the nesting bird, after I had forbidden him to hunt for the nest, he made a point of surprising her every time she stole in with a piece of grass, chuckling delightedly, 'Ha. Caught ee that time, Missis.'

Presently I began again on the subject we had dropped. 'Of course Nancy's different. But not nearly so much because of her fears about inheriting her father's queerness as because people have worried her all her life.'

Dick, accustomed to conversation which spins out to the length of a day's work, returned to the point immediately. 'She'm different because her dad were mazed.' He paused to gather together his argument. 'You got to terrify folks a bit when they'm like that. Don't, they think they'm better'n the rest.'

He continued his trap-setting in silence. He had exerted himself, beyond his usual extent, to give an answer: his conviction inherited from generations who kept order in their small communities by constant assertion of conformity and distrust of the unusual.

When Dick was young, if a man from the next village came into the Bell he was thrown out, not from personal ill-will, but in affirmation of village solidarity; and the same treatment was expected and meted out to Dick and his mates when they invaded the neighbouring village inn. Under such rough government practical kindness was not wanting, but the weaker members knew their place and paid for their inability to assert their village's good name in the acceptance of half-jocular, half-malicious tormenting.

'Have ee heard Nance is coming home?'

Long ago Dick and I recognized certain unalterable differences of outlook, and I doubt if he had any idea of changing the subject. By his way of thinking he was pursuing it.

'Jim 've got a week's holiday coming. They'm going to stop at Rackenfords'. Lot o' coming and going.' He elaborated when I said I had not heard. 'Mrs Belstone—Steve's missis—have been over to Mrs Rackenford a time or two, fixing something up, a cure or something, for Nance—to do with thik trouble of her dad's, shouldn't wonder.'

I did not ask him how he knew. It is not possible to tell how people in clustered, isolated dwellings know what each does. But they do. Trained in lifelong association with one another, suspicion and observation fused into an extra sense have taught them how to interpret a word, a look, a change of dress, the slightest deviation from usual habit. They call it putting two and two together, and probably few would deny its hint of malice. But it shares, in some degree, the sensitivity of the twitching nose at the mouth of a burrow, scenting the wind for danger.

No doubt Dick hoped that my face would add something to his little store of information about Nancy's homecoming, and if I had known anything perhaps it would have, under his expert scrutiny. But I knew nothing, though I wondered whether he had made up his own version of the motive for Cicely's visits from Stephen's wife.

 # 60

In the still, sunlit early morning there is no sound but the shouting of birds, and in the evening no other sound in the lane but one's own footfall and the birds' song.

Joining the exultation from trees and hedges, curlews who have left their marshy hunting grounds for the domestic safety of dry hayfields pour watery songs over their nesting places; plovers, forgetting their homely absorption in building, rise with the least earthly of all bird calls, and above us all, riding against the sky, a pair of buzzards answer one another with the voice of savage cats.

Near the house sings a thrush, which as part of its song imitates a mallard. Many times I have been deceived, this year and in years gone by, and its croaking, provocative song brings before me, more pointedly than all the others, the familiar sight of spring in voluptuous, shouting, extravagant ascendancy.

This is cuckoo weather, once recognized by a milky sky in which it is hard to distinguish the veiled blue from the soft clouds that have no beginning and no end, pastures hazed with dew, and cattle lying in the dewy shade; and over the still air, across veiled fields and greening hedges, comes the cuckoo's song. One day, suddenly, buttercups will cover the pastures, and milkmaids, and daisies with white petals rose-bordered when they close at night.

With new foliage the sound of trees has changed, each according to its habit. The sturdy, knotted twigs of an oak rock a little, answering the breeze, the short-stemmed leaves held rigid. Young elm leaves grow on stiff, thin twigs, and their movement is swaying, and their voice purls in the wind. But in light airs every leaf of a beech is astir: they hang on such slender, pliable stalks that each leaf flutters singly, still pleated with long furling, on boughs that rise and fall and rise again with the rustle of silk, softly fingering the breeze.

The shadow of a cider-apple tree is never complete on the grass. Because of the grotesque entwining of its branches it is dense in one place and lets full sunlight through in large O's in another, and with the branches' rhythm the shade continually changes. Here and there in the orchard of bent and slanting trees one leans so steeply that its roots are half pulled out of the earth and it rests on the ground. Yet even these put forth clustered, shining leaves, and among them the apples of the new season form beneath brown and shrivelled flowers.

In the still latitude between the flickering leaves and their glancing shade Stephen Belstone's wife inspected my first eight goslings, advertised in the local paper this morning, and sold to her over the telephone before breakfast; and while she considered them we played a conversational game usual on such occasions: an exchange of talk played like a hand of cards, politely deferring the moment of getting down to business.

If we had been strangers, or almost strangers, for no-one in the neighbourhood is quite unheard of, the game would have followed a pattern well known to us both. Each in turn would throw down a scrap of information, the other following suit with picture card or plain until at last, gathering up our tricks—a handful of knowledge of one another's family, holding, stock and experience—we would turn our attention to the sale.

But we knew too much about each other to play the game

with its customary subtlety, and too little to meet on the friendly footing of relations. During all the years of the brothers' estrangement nothing important can have happened on either farm without the news threading its way through neighbours' talk. So we played a hand of polite exchanges, and presently George joined us, settling down with the alert passivity of a well-trained dog, letting our talk see-saw over his head.

Only when Richeldis passed me her cheque book, following local custom, so that I could fill in my price, he intervened: 'Lucy can't write in a small space, now,' and added, possibly to cover up the baldness of his disclosure: 'It's a bit old-fashioned, you know, passing cheque books round.'

'I am old-fashioned,' Richeldis said.

'I know,' said George.

Sensibly, she did not press for the source of his agreement. Probably he could not have enlightened her, anyway. Our histories and habits are the foundation of the children's experience, laid down, haphazard, on chance bits of conversation overheard. Long after a man is dead, if a neighbour remembers that he used to sow his peas or shallots or spring cabbages on a certain date another will agree that he was a very punctual man: if his dinner was late he would throw the cooking pot out of the window. Our word-of-mouth biographies depend on the vigour of our idiosyncrasies, and they are built up day by day out of gossip.

Not that gossip has found much to improvise on about Stephen's wife. No sensational discovery has ever prolonged anyone's thirst at the Bell or held up a washing day. But that is not to say that comment has passed her by. George would have heard how she peppered a neighbour's trespassing pigs with her husband's shotgun, and threatened to do the same to a young woman sent out to inspect her dairy. Exploiting to the full a child's freedom of the countryside he may have dropped in to sample her hospitality, and have had tea in the kitchen shared with a pig or two that has been brought in as a nestle-tripe and has remained underfoot with lambs brought up on the bottle, and hens that have gained an entry after some casualty and still bustle in to lay. No one knows for certain, enjoying 'a proper old-fashioned tea,' that cats lapped the cream while it set, or were chased off the warm dough while it rose in a bowl by the fire. Clean meat never fattened a pig. They say that the hams, tied to a string, soak in the stream for a day before they are boiled, where cattle drowse the afternoons away and slobber water among the Aylesburys sleeping head on wing.

Whenever her name crops up in conversation some such tale will be told about Richeldis, with a semblance of disapprobation, but, like a mother recounting the exploits of an unusual child, with some concealed pride, all the same. For the name that has meandered down generations of daughters of her family—stilled on a tombstone, springing up again among the christenings in a parish register, pronounced in full on a wedding day, yelled 'Cheldis' above the sound of scrubbing, worn smooth and homely like a silver spoon used for stirring porridge—owes its long inheritance, as her eccentricities do, to some of the best land in England: the red land that has enabled men to hand on an inheritance of small fields even during bankrupting agricultural depressions, and to summon up resistance to withstand the tempting offers of land-hungry townsmen in the golden days of recovery.

There are other such names in the neighbourhood—Cicely's is one of them—heirlooms handed down with housewifely education to daughters who in each generation have turned up their noses at some of the labours their grandmothers thought nothing of—soap-making, candle-dipping, and the face-scorching operation of raking out the ashes from a white-hot bread oven—yet retaining a long memory of discarded crafts. Entrenched in their kitchens, fortified by years of experience, stored recipes and remedies, common sense and old wives' tales, deferring only to the demands of the seasons, they have forged their armour of domestic autocracy.

Only Richeldis appears to have trudged, without a glance at four centuries of husbandry, straight from the days when a man measured his land by the area oxen could plough; and time by sunlight creeping to a notch on a doorpost, or the position of a shadow on a field. She belongs with the figures in a tapestry stooping over a harvest field, distinguished from the men only by feminine clothes. She has come straight from the briar that formed the stock on which Cicely's and my mother's kind were grafted.

Some say she has been a drag on Stephen: the unlaid hedges and dilapidated gates, the hand-to-mouth manner of their farming, is put down to her lack of household management. Then others will say that it is not her fault; she would like everything smooth-running: no dung sold off the farm or hasty sales to settle pressing bills; but he's too keen on horses. According to the tide of local opinion each is tumbled or uplifted sympathetically on waves of neighbourly judgement.

When she had driven away with the goslings, crated and squawking indignantly in the back of the car, George came back with me to fold up the wire of the pen, and while he was thus engaged he pored over the finds the afternoon had brought him, after the time-honoured manner of children, in a soliloquy of questions.

'I wonder what she really came for, Luce. I don't expect she truly wanted the goslings, do you?'

'She said, when she went, you must see more of each other. Did you notice that? It'd be awfully useful.' (It is funny, the way children like to find practical advantage in their speculations.) 'She's a sort of vet, did you know? She makes all sorts of herb things for animals—and people too, only they don't much like other people knowing they try them, because they'd be laughed at nowadays. D'you think they'd be any good?

'I expect Mr Belstone'll be glad to know his brother again. I mean it's pretty uncomfortable not speaking to your brother, well, for long, anyway. Specially if you're a farmer; you're useful to each other. I think families ought to stick together, don't you?

'You know, I don't expect she'd ever have come if you hadn't gone half blind, do you Luce? She's not a bad old trot, d'you think? Not'—he experimented—'a bad old tart at all.'

There is something that suggests laughter in the aqueous shade of rippling orchard grass.

62

In the middle of the afternoon a car drove into the yard, and as I went out to find out who was there Father came in through the field gate, and I recognized the voice from the car as the vet's.

All the morning I had kept an eye on Cleo—the old phrases linger—four days overdue with calf and making apparent efforts to calve during the last two. At dinner-time Father said that one foot had appeared, but before he went back to the fields it had receded.

I guessed that while Father's pride would not allow him to telephone until he must it had allowed him to mention that he was in for a difficult calving, while he chatted over the hedge to the vet as he passed on his round. That would explain why the vet, who has a fund of stories kept for the ladies, of a different kind from the ones that raise sudden laughter when he is alone with Father and Dick, having, also, a strong sense of occasion, briskly ordered a bucket of water and soap and a towel, instead of lingering to tell me his latest; and immediately an atmosphere of urgency invaded the yard.

When I brought out the things he had asked for he was in the pen with Father, examining the cow which was soberly chewing the cud.

'We must try to save cow and calf,' he said.

Cleo's milky breath caressed our faces. She looked pensively round at him and continued chewing. Professional touches are lost on animals; but among the vet's hard-headed clients, who deal continually with emergencies only a shade less serious than those they are forced to call him in for, a little professional bravado, backing resource and skill, colours the occasion and adds to their money's worth when it comes to paying the bill.

I went and stood by the cow's head, laying a hand on her neck, talking to her as she had learnt to expect when she was a calf, when George named her Cleopatra.

The vet took off his jacket in silence. His bedside manner fitted him as snugly as his gaiters. A year ago, when he came to help with a calving, I did not dream that it was the last time I should see him in his waistcoat and well-cut breeches, washing his hands and arms and the two lengths of rope and two small wooden batons that he took from his bag; but I noticed, then, how white his hair had grown since we first knew him—as white as my father's; and I wondered whether, while each of us was sure to have observed the others' ageing, we had all spared ourselves consideration of our own.

With thirty years of experience I waited for the moment when, rolling back his sleeves, he would take on a sociable air, as dentists do before beginning their work. I heard him pull his mackintosh overall out of the bag, and shaking it out thrust his arms through its crackling folds, then, 'Well,' he said, 'it looks as though we'll have a fine day for the County Show tomorrow.' His voice was slightly distorted; evidently he was tying the string in the neck at the back of his overall.

We chatted for a moment. Then he was ready, taking a wide stance on his stocky legs, and I knew that his left hand would be on the cow's rump for leverage while with deft, searching movements he found the calf's forefeet and attached the ropes' ends to them. He would wind each free end round a baton and hand one to Father.

When they had arranged themselves, stirring the brittle straw on the floor of the pen with their feet, 'Pull, Sir, pull for all you're worth,' he said.

As they heaved, Cleo stretched her neck forward, but she gave no sign of pain. The men hauled, relaxed, and hauled.

The vet handed Father both batons while he guided the calf's head, and with a mighty effort they pulled its body free. Grey and wet it would be, seeming lifeless as it landed on the straw with a thud.

The vet knelt and worked its forelegs—stiffly they would move in his hands, like pistons—then it breathed and moved its head. The vet added his last professional touch. Without another glance at the prostrate little body, 'A heifer,' he said.

Normality flowed back into the yard, and awareness of the time of day. A cat, emerging from the black interior of the barn, the first-comer for milking, chattered at the house-martins swooping and fidgeting in the sunny air, choosing their nesting places under the house eaves. Muttering testily, blowzy with sleep, it would stretch indolently, too lazy to project its avaricious glance as far as the noisy birds.

While he was putting on his jacket the vet told me the story he had postponed at our meeting, about a farmer's little son who asked his mother whether it was true that angels had wings, like fowls. 'What,' the child asked then, 'do they do with broody angels?'

When I was back in the kitchen I heard Father's rare laugh, and wondered whether the story that had changed hands was of animal husbandry told with a human slant, or about neighbours, expressed in veterinary terms.

63

George came with us to the County Show. Walking up the hill field to the show ground, 'It looks like the Field of the Cloth of Gold,' he said. And so it might, in the windy sunshine; massed pavilions with banners flying against the sky.

One of the company climbing the hill with us, putting his own construction on the remark, agreed, with the stolid jocularity farm workers reserve for the assertion that everyone but themselves harvests a fortune from the land. 'So 'tis, for some. A field o' gold. That's a gude un.'

He passed George's observation on to his neighbours, with his reply, and George, unexpectedly, found himself to be the author of a wisecrack.

Moving along avenues of stands held by everyone who sells anything to farmers, down lanes of penned beasts that had been judged, in and out of tents laden with the hot smell of canvas and trodden grass, with the cheerful, loitering, shouldering crowd, we basked in the atmosphere of high farming, criticizing, vicariously owning, speculating, disbelieving.

A little boy patted the flank of a prize bull lying and chewing the cud. 'Er's too fat to be comfortable,' he said.

In the days when I could spare a glance for everything I used to be amused to see how slowly the bulls could walk in the Grand Parade in the ring, as though foot would hardly follow foot. Led by the rings in their noses, wearing on their halters the rosettes they had won—in some cases blinking through the ribbons of several—dawdling with huge shoulders hunched, their broad backs dwindling to narrow buttocks, they move at tortoise pace, the cows of their breed led on halters behind them, a docile harem.

Now I find that it is the homely things I miss seeing most: the fowls in the poultry tent, brilliant White Wyandottes, and Light Sussex birds with collars like ladies' feather boas, shampooed for the show—washed and rinsed in blue, and towelled the way of the feathers and set in a hamper to dry by the fire, and turned as they dry—and the eggs, dead white or golden, red-brown and speckled, all finished with a waxen polish; and honey, clear and dark in beautifully filled combs; and beeswax set in moulds, smelling of flowers.

We met Mrs Shenley, composed and exquisite among the thrusting crowd. George told her about the joke he had not intended to make about the Field of the Cloth of Gold.

'I always think nothing matters as long as one keeps one's sense of humour,' she said.

On the way home George asked: 'Have you ever known anyone who could charm away ringworm and warts and things, Luce?'

'Yes,' I said.

'Have you ever known a witch?'

'No. That's asking too much. Have you?'

'Of course not. But they say old ladies used to turn into hares—to get away from gamekeepers and people like that—and if a gamekeeper wounded a hare one of the old girls'd go about with a bandage on. And you know they wouldn't cross a broomstick because they'd lose their power? Well, once some chaps put a broomstick across an old girl's door and she couldn't go out, even to relieve herself. What d'you think about it, Luce?'

'Well, I suppose those tales were made up for some purpose. They enhanced the reputation of people who had some useful powers.'

'Have you ever heard of people wearing flowers to keep away illnesses and things?'

'I've heard of similar things. Where did you learn all this?'

'Oh, I heard someone talking about it,' he said.

64

'My father wasn't anything like a doctor, was he?'
'I haven't known many,' I said. 'He certainly wasn't much like one's idea of a doctor.'

Pamela was in her mother's old workroom upstairs, a room that once enjoyed the distinction of the front of the house before the place was turned back to front, matching other farmhouses where the back door, leading into the yard, is naturally the main thoroughfare. She was rummaging through drawers in search of the boys' savings books, which she hoped would disclose enough money to buy new tyres for the tractor.

The floor was bare, and even to my dim sight it was clear that the place where a carpet had been in the old days was still unstained and unpolished. The bed was unmade, and from the open drawers of a chest clothes spilled and swooned together on to the floor. Several panes of glass were missing from the window and I knew, from past observation, that below us, on the conservatory roof, hardly a pane would be whole. But beyond the wilderness of neglected garden cows were noisily tearing grass, and I guessed that the herd grazed, in the pink of condition, a pasture as scrupulously cared for as themselves.

'This is my dream house,' Pamela said.

I sat on the floor; there were no chairs. Only her mother's davenport remained of the old furniture in the room where boxes and laundry baskets, overflowing with remainders from village jumble sales, Christmas parties, whist drives and fêtes, used to wait for the tide of parish activity to wash them into circulation again, and a sewing machine, clutching in its teeth some dangling object of apparel in process of alteration, once gave the room its name. Though whenever Pamela and I went there her mother seems to have been sitting at her davenport with three purses, an account book and three towers of money before her.

Looking up, she would slant her gaze at us over her reading spectacles, and as soon as she had disposed of us, while we still dawdled about, would return to the job we had interrupted, frowning at the account book, counting the money, and writing the sum of each pile on a slip of paper which she returned with the cash to the purses.

One day I asked Pamela what the pieces of paper were for.

'To keep people from taking the money,' she said. 'If the amount's written down they couldn't take it without altering the writing, could they?'

'Has anyone ever taken any, then?'

'Of course not,' she said; then added, instructively: 'you shouldn't put temptation in people's way.'

In those days, though she jibbed and kicked when her mother tried to break her in to the uses of domesticity, occasionally she would perform dazzling evolutions for my benefit.

'Of course, if anyone did take anything, Mother would write "I know who is taking my money" and put that in the purse with the amount, and that would soon stop it.'

I pondered for some time whether this afterthought was make-believe or really her mother's intention. The oblique methods of the gentry, in contrast to our unsubtle approaches, were a recurring surprise to me.

When I asked what the three purses were for, one, I was told, was for housekeeping, one for personal expenses, the other for extras. Years later I realized that the one for extras continually robbed the other two; hence, no doubt, the frown bent over the account book. For many a local child, rocketing from village to grammar school, or setting out on a first job, escaped the cruel distinction of shabbiness or unsuitability through the contrivance of the third purse.

It seems, now, that all the rooms at the Old Vicarage were furnished with faded brown curtains. Sunlight, glancing off bleached brown hangings, lay on the windowsills, the worn carpets and faded surfaces of inherited furniture, smooth as treacle; and on winter evenings the light of lamps glimmering on brown velvet curtains lent the rooms the tobacco colouring and sense of immutability of oil paintings.

I used to wonder whatever made the Doctor choose to settle in a house with none of the modern improvements that he would have found in the village. When he took over the practice, on his release from army medical service at the end of the 1914 war, electricity may only have been on the way, but the old doctor's house in the village was lit by gas. Probably his wife took a fancy to this one, deprived of a vicar by the union of our parish with the next. She would have been in her element as a vicar's wife, and she revived the character of the deserted vicarage with the same enthusiasm, the devoted abandon of the amateur, that her daughter applies now to turning it into a farmhouse.

The only house I ever went into that compared with it was the Mowbrays'. That had the same air of comfortable disregard for effect, the same casual assumption that everything in it was valuable far beyond mere utility. But at the Doctor's all was busy and orderly; at the Judge's the atmosphere was grander in some subtle way that was above orderliness or even punctuality. If you happened to be at the Mowbrays' just before a meal-time Mr Silvester, unobtrusive as a cat, would come to announce that it was served, would be acknowledged with a gesture, and then, apparently, be forgotten. At the Doctor's one of the maids thumped on a gong and everyone hurried to their places while she put the dog out of the room, lest it should affront decorum by cadging. At the Mowbrays' a foxhound, resting its muzzle on the table, might embrace with its tongue anything it fancied.

I suppose the time-table of the Doctor's perfectly run house was arranged to fit in with the practice. In my young days it did not seem so; his coming and going were so casual. No air of urgency ever surrounded him; such disturbances as there were centred on parish festivities, or the maids who pursued a housekeeping calendar as clearly signposted as the farming year, or the suppressed news of some village scandal whose earthquake tremors, manifested in suddenly closed doors and abruptly silenced adult conversation, tantalizingly fissured the walls of ignorance confining Pamela and me, but never opened chasms wide enough to let us into the secret.

In our kitchen, the heart of the house, wood fires and the just discernible astringency of hanging bacon, the whiff of the seasons that came in with us every time we opened the door, composed the uncomplicated home atmosphere; at the Mowbrays' a bouquet rested on the air, a subtle reminiscence of cigar smoke and saddle leather; the Old Vicarage was filled with the exhalations of busyness.

To the unjaded nose of childhood I suppose every house has a special smell, charged with warnings and reassurances, invitations and barriers. At the Old Vicarage there was a place at the top of the stairs, in the passage that led to the schoolroom, where on certain days you could tell what time of year it was. The smell of hot beeswax and turpentine melting into home-made furniture polish spiralled up from the kitchen to herald the springtime of the domestic year; the ant-sting fumes of pickling vinegar succeeded the satin-sweetness of boiling jam at the end of summer; winter came in with the foggy, clothy ripeness of simmering Christmas puddings. Each contributed to the climate of disciplined comfort in the house where no one except the Doctor ate butter with jam, though there was plenty of both, or salad as well as pickles, or pickles and mustard; and no one tied a new label on to a parcel if the unused half of an old one could be found, or opening a parcel cut the string.

A dado of brown hessian masked the wallpaper of the back staircase, which we used to go up to the schoolroom. It would be too decisive to say that one could smell it; rather the nose detected its fibrous surface, and as clearly as though its threads had spelt out 'Waste not, that others may not want,' it symbolized the ruses and economies, conservations and self-denials in the midst of plenty, that the Doctor's wife devised to maintain the resources of her third purse.

I am astonished now to find how vaguely I remember her appearance. She was too far beyond my experience for consideration; I had nothing to measure her by. Only her gaze, as she bent over her desk, is fixed for ever, possibly because it had some unexpected suggestion of defiance in it. Otherwise I see her always hurrying, dark and spare, about her household supervision and her good works. She was devoid of tact; diplomacy was as unnatural to her as to a bird. Infinitely benevolent, without knowing what she did, she would send missiles hurtling through the palisade of reserve that growing children build to defend their privacy.

'Are you looking forward to being confirmed . . . remembering to say your prayers at night . . . to clean your teeth in the morning?' Her enquiries sent the children she was fitting out with new clothes flying behind barricades of churlishness. But she did not seem to notice, any more than she seemed to care or know what she ate while she picked absent-mindedly at the excellent meals she ordered; and I wonder whether Pamela, whose tawny magnificence derives nothing from her mother's compact neatness, inherited from her her disdain of superficialities, though their idea of triviality is almost opposite.

The Doctor I remember clearly, for deluded by his apparent simplicity I accepted him, without further consideration, as a 'joky article', protracting our breaks between lessons with stories allegedly of his own experience or of his legendary companions at Cambridge—stories which we often discovered later in old numbers of *Punch*—until his wife hunted us back to the schoolroom, like a busy terrier stirring up rats.

On the first morning that I went to the Vicarage for lessons I was asked by Pamela, as we went upstairs: 'Are you Cambridge or Oxford?'

Possibly it was the day of the Boat Race, an event which had not previously attracted my attention.

'I'm not sure,' I said. Self-defence warned me, for the first of many times, that the Vicarage was not only strange country, it was Pamela's home ground.

'I'm Cambridge,' she said, 'of course. You're whichever your father went to.'

'I'll ask,' I said. 'I expect mine's been to one or the other; or somewheres else.'

It was before the days of Gloucester Wrangways's nicknaming, but our bent for preserving the remembrance of one another's excursions is not new.

'Somewhere,' corrected Pamela, and put the finishing touch to my mystification by adding: 'there is nowhere else.'

I stayed at the Vicarage for luncheon. Getting no bias from the answers to my questions at home in the evening I was Cambridge from that day, and later experience revealed that the maids, the gardener, even the dog at the Vicarage, were Cambridge too.

I became a chameleon. At home, after Mother and I had dished up a meal and I had jumped up a few times to fetch things that I had forgotten to put on the table, we would rest our elbows comfortably on the cloth between helpings and argue about whether it was Church or Stream Field that had been dunged in the autumn; Whitefoot or Jetty who had been fortuitously served, when she broke out three months ago, by the Shenleys' Guernsey bull. At the Vicarage our food was placed before us by Cicely's sister, who was parlourmaid then, and I thanked her extravagantly until I learnt to imitate the polite impassiveness of the others.

At home we touched extremes of indulgence and hardship. Likes and dislikes were pandered to as though they were physical necessities: 'Lucy never touches fat.' 'Father won't look at an onion.' Everything was discussed among us all, good deals and bad, disputes between neighbours, misfortunes, disasters. We lived cheek by jowl, and fostered our nearness with continual demands on one another for help, condolence or congratulation. Only the emergency of safeguarding our livelihood wiped out our emotional interdependence: if any of the beasts was in danger from sickness or foul weather or its own wrong-headedness, or a crop in jeopardy, we laboured regardless of discomfort, hurts or personal distastes, like the crew of a lifeboat.

But across the road I made the changes in demeanour that my new surroundings required, with uncritical acquiescence that was in direct contrast to Pamela's unyielding resistance.

One does not eat cheese off the tip of one's knife.

'Why not?' asked Pamela, my example appealing instantly by its rustic simplicity.

Because one might cut one's lip, we were told. It would have been madness to tell Pamela that a thing was 'not done'.

Speaking when I was not spoken to, and often on subjects considered highly unsuitable, I gradually discovered restraint, and a new kind of separateness which was applauded as a sense of responsibility, though nothing depended on us children: the breadwinning, the meals, the housekeeping, were no concern of ours. Duty took the place of necessity; observances and prohibitions, disciplines and graces, the place of the makeshifts and ingenious devices and slogging hard work that I shared in meeting the demands of the animals, the land, and family well-being at home.

Our book-learning was fitted into a meshwork of homely and social instruction following the pattern of the education Pamela's mother had had; and though our schoolroom lessons took up an exactly measured part of our time, memory has spared surprisingly little for our governess, a schoolmistress who had retired to the village, whose personality had melted into the all-managing preponderance of the Doctor's wife.

Pamela's mother conducted the prayers that began our day—her congregation doubled by the rustling entrance of the maids—and after two hours of lessons collected us for a walk, when we covered a set distance along one of the lanes, never stopping to look over a gate, never scrutinizing a growing crop, but making conversation. Our afternoon lessons were broken by intervals during which she taught us sewing, or handed us over to the peppery old specialist in the kitchen for a spell of cookery, or to the housemaid who, though she must have guessed that I had first-hand experience in her subject, generously forbore from comment while I fiddled about in a ladylike way.

I do not remember trying to deceive anyone: like the rest of that life, with its rituals and ceremonies, even household chores had an unfamiliar look. Believing, at first, that our brisk morning excursions must be an extension of the art of walking, I began by pointing my feet and putting them down toes first.

Whenever he was about, the Doctor put up a smoke-screen of anecdote, camouflaging my homespun awkwardness and Pamela's discordance. At first his tales were incomprehensible to me. He seldom spoke of his hospital training: Cambridge was the background of almost all of them, and it was some time before it dawned on me that a Gyp and a Bulldog were not possible opponents in a dog fight, nor a Bedder a racy abbreviation of Bedlington terrier.

I suppose he thought us capable of visualizing him as the young Blood he presented to us in the tall stories he told in the first person. It was beyond me. I vaguely imagined the cropped grey hair some indeterminate colour, but if I made any further attempt to rejuvenate him I was baffled immediately by the rather prominent grey eyes clouded with an unemphatic expression I never tried to fathom, and only attempt, now, to define as observant anonymity.

It was as though he had found his way by mistake into that house, spinning on its merry-go-round of activity; by accident taken his place among the medalled walkers in the Armistice Day procession into church.

If he talked to his wife about the practice in front of us children he adopted an allusive way of speaking, giving his patients classical names which defeated our curiosity. When his car broke down, as it did with obstinate regularity because he refused to learn how to cope with even its minor disorders, he matched its versatility with ingenious diagnosis. Sclerosis dimmed its lights; a disarticulation of its spine brought him home, one day, driving slowly backwards from the Moor; its runaway precipitation, when the brakes failed, he described as a festinating gait.

At one time Pamela and I tried to get our homework done by asking him to translate our Latin for us—child's play for him; he had read Classics before medicine. But our guile was confounded. His talent for interchange mingled Caesar's warfare with reminiscence of the Western Front, and the Roman and British armies fused inextricably as 'our chaps'.

None of us appreciated him. We mistook his humour for frivolity, his detachment for irresponsibility. It needed no acute perception to see that his wife, busy and affectionate, regarded as the chief of her domestic concerns her duty to keep his meditative gaze bent on his livelihood.

He was nothing like the robust idea of a country doctor typified by his predecessor. The old doctor used to ride round his practice tapping on windows with his whip, prescribing castor oil or embrocation or cough mixture, from the saddle; and because almost everyone came under his authority sometime his position in the adult world was very like the schoolmaster's from the point of view of the children. He was respected, slightly feared, and deceived as often as was possible and expedient. His medicines were swallowed or applied as a second string to remedies of herbs and charms and animal fragments which were assiduously concealed.

When Pamela's father died he left a collection of recipes for the home-made medicines and semi-magical cures with which his patients had fortified his prescribed treatments. Now, defeated in their attempts to do justice to his impartiality in allowing their concoctions to go, as it were, hand in hand with his, when they speak of him they do not say he was a good doctor, or even a bad one; but fumbling among the thrifty currency of their esteem will venture: 'He were a gude man. A proper gentleman.'

There is never, at any other time of year, the glow and luxuriance of now. Flowers toss and shoulder one another along the banks and nod from the hedge tops, and deep beds of nettles conceal, in a few days, any garden tool carelessly left about. Now only the nights can still the competitive whistle and shout of blackbird and thrush, the wood pigeons' repetition and the small birds' undersong.

Even one of the outdoor hens, a spinster since her hatching, has responded to the sappy, voluptuous time, and conducts an imaginary family round the yard. I can hear her, clucking maternally, kicking the dirt strongly with each foot, stepping back to search among the disturbed dust and calling her phantom young, brought forth from a clutch of infertile eggs.

Flashes of memory settle on details that escaped remark before, which must have been noticed and passed by: the spoked jewellery of cow parsley in the lane banks, the tendrils of frizzed hair that anchor the vetch, cocksfoot grass upthrusting the toes of a fowl.

I met George in the lane, searching among the flowers on the bank.

'Nancy's back. She's coming over to you tomorrow,' he said. 'I was on my way to see you in a minute. Mother's found a piece of poetry she thought you'd like.' He pronounced the word 'poitry', affectedly, as I used to at his age; but he read, from the scrap of paper that he edged out of his pocket, in the artless tones of childhood, emotionless as the treble voices that soar in choirs to cathedral roofs.

> '*They have no song, the sedges dry,*
> *And still they sing.*
> *It is within my breast they sing,*
> *As I pass by.*
> *Within my breast they touch a string,*
> *They wake a sigh.*
> *There is but sound of sedges dry;*
> *In me they sing.*'

While he underwent the contortions, in returning the paper to his pocket, that he had knotted himself into in extracting it, 'I suppose, in a way, you see things that aren't there,' he suggested, 'and don't see things that are. There's a sow thistle in your barley field, Luce.'

I thought at first that this was a reflection on our husbandry, but it seems he has turned herbalist; for when I apologized for it frivolously, he volunteered: 'In the Middle Ages milk taken from the stalks, and given in drink, was thought beneficial to those that were short-winded and had the wheezing.'

I asked whether he had found any flowers useful for his purpose on the bank.

'Yes,' he said, 'bugle, singularly good for all hurts of the body; and herb benet, of potent might in the assuaging of bodily pains, an effectual help in things spiritual against the wiles of evil spirits or the influence of wicked men.' But so far he had searched in vain for betony, a protection against evil spirits which, taken beforehand, hindered drunkenness, and afterwards, cleared the head.

'Where in the world did you get all this from?' I asked.

'From Mrs Rackenford. She lent me a book. As a matter of fact she knows someone who uses it.' His casual tone approached a moment of disclosure.

'Who?'

'Your aunt. Mrs Belstone, who bought the goslings. She and Mrs Rackenford have found some flowers that will keep

Nancy from going funny. They thought it would make her come back and live with you. But she won't, because it wouldn't stop people taking the mickey out of her, would it?'

'I suppose not,' I said. 'How do you know all this?'

He prevaricated. 'You don't have to worry, though, because Mrs Belstone and her husband are going to help you out on your farm when you need it. Blood,' he concluded sententiously, 'is thicker than water.'

'You don't say! How on earth do you know so much about it?'

'I was just mucking about in Rackenfords' yard when they were talking about it indoors.'

66

Nancy came to the farm this morning and I took her out to the field to show her the two geese on their nests, Hetty in the goosehouse, Kate in a corner of the heifers' shed. Each sat down a month ago to brood eight eggs.

We stood in the doorway of the goosehouse, with the early sunshine warming our backs.

'What's Hetty doing?'

'Laying her head down, hiding.'

'And now?' We went a few steps nearer.

'Standing. And she've eight little goslings there. Good old gander.'

We visited Kate, who repeated Hetty's motions: the secret protective lowering of the head; the hissing, threatening stance. Nancy counted the chicks once, and then again.

'She've nine,' she reported, and for a moment we relished the magic of the situation. We both knew at once that the goose had laid another egg after she had sat down to brood, but both of us, I suspect, were tempted to defer the solution, telling our neighbours that we had had two goslings from one egg.

For we have an affinity for the miraculous. Down the generations inventive minds have intruded discoveries on the countryman's methods; and innovations, whether in the interests of cropping or stock-raising, harvesting or working down a tilth, all have a potentiality for sweeping away a lifetime's experience in favour of systems for ousting craft of hand by machine work, and of threatening the farm worker's expectation of a livelihood by designs for replacing two or three men's keep with the wages of one. So we treasure any hints that Nature drops of a secret or two up her sleeve, and if we can twist them into proverbs pointing out our belief that she will use them to counter interference we do. But even without self-interest we have an innate delight in the marvellous. It is so ingrained that the six months' abrasion that has fined Nancy down to the pattern acceptable in her new environment appears to have left it undiminished.

She had brought me a set of table mats, which, she said, were for standing wine glasses on—surely the strangest present I have ever had; and she explained their advantages in preventing cocktail stains from spoiling the furniture.

There was an occasion, thirty years ago, when the Doctor bought a new hat. Straight out of an Exeter shop the brown felt looked smooth, too smooth, and not shaped as yet to his head as the old one had been. It would have been hard to say whether it was too big or too small; the only certainty was that it did not fit, and that it was out of keeping with his old tweed suit. The contrast perfectly matched, in unsuitability, Nancy's ill-fitting semblance of sophistication and her homely pleasure in the geese, who brooded their families all day in nests of down and curled feathers and in the evening brought them out beneath the drooping, moving, rustling elms.

At the time I was dismayed by her prattle about washing machines, hairdressing, and the smart brands of everything to eat or use; quite different from her fancies in the past for the novelties offered in catalogues. Speculated upon against the background of her home and ours their appeal was superficial, this taste seemed to be for icing and no cake. I was dismayed, too, by her unquestioning satisfaction with the new part she found herself playing: 'I like new things to eat; Jim's on the bigoty side,' and her amused contempt for the ways she has left behind: 'There I used to be, swip-swapping the old flat-irons on the fire while Jim waited for a clean shirt.'

I forgot what a desperate thing it must have been to be hauled up by the roots to exchange the companionship of a few lifelong associates for the surface familiarity of suburban life.

Her mother, it seems, after the manner of old people, has made no attempt to acclimatize herself to her new surroundings, and simply rests on the surface of the family's activities taking what comes, as a tree brought down in a storm will lie in the current of a Dartmoor stream, keeping roots in the bank and lifting branches, still bearing leaves, above the water piling against its prostrate trunk.

But Nancy, determined to make a success of Jim's new venture undertaken for her sake, and possibly with some idea that shortcomings on her part might jeopardize it, has erred on the other side, and has evidently plunged into the thick of her neighbours' discussions and entertainments, gratefully accepting all the fashionable instruction pressed upon her. In compensation for the merriment provoked by her ingenuousness she must often have thought of how she would be able to queen it over us here; and which of us who were wearied by her half-boastful, half-patronizing excitability could be sure that we should have emerged unscathed by the pin-prick goading of minute, successive humiliations, or have allowed it to penetrate no more than skin-deep.

Giving her news of our friends I told her how I had made a meat pie for Mr Luppett, not long ago, to give him a change from his own cooking, as his neighbours do from time to time; and how he, as a tribute to the memory of his late wife's talent, had returned it half eaten—as he frequently does—saying that it gave him indigestion.

'Ignorant thing,' said Nancy, slipping into the vernacular in defence of my self-esteem. 'If you'd made me a pie I couldn't eat, I'd have buried it and said it was lovely.'

67

Everything is in keeping: the rippling fields with swaying flowers, hedgerow trees in heavy leaf, and in the lanes the heavy scent of elder, flower of thunder-weather and hay-time. Yet no hay is being made. There is something sickly in the sunshine and restless in the wind that disturbs the leaves of trees moving branches uneasily. House-martins chatter as they weave and twist above the grass flowers. Cows come back heavily to the yard in the middle of the day, with buzzing clouds of flies about their heads. No weather for letting the cream idle, neighbours say.

To us that advice is all that is necessary to describe the day: when cream scalding on the low heat of the stove turns sour before its surface has time to honeycomb. So, now that I cannot watch it on the faster heat that is needed, I scald no cream in this weather, and miss, on the following day, the pleasure of skimming: cutting round the crisp edge against the pan with a knife, quartering the crumpled surface with two strokes, north to south, west to east, lifting off each quarter on the skimmer, steady-handed to avoid drowning it in the white milk beneath; repeating the motions of my mother and all the women of my family before me in a job they could have done blindfolded, and which my hands will follow through now unerringly with linked movements bridging gaps once taken at a leap by the eye. Continuity has become indispensable even in everyday things: a substitute for seeing.

Tired of pottering with the machinery he would far rather have abused for breaking down in the hayfield, half-way through the afternoon Father came in to suggest that we should go over to Stephen's. It was in keeping with his safeguarding concealment of expression that the casualness of his proposal overlooked half a lifetime of no more than face-saving acknowledgement of his brother in public places, and any necessity to explain that George's conclusions, based on eavesdropping, deserved investigation.

All my life the other farm, Stephen's, has been the example of perfection, simply because it is the place where my father and I were born. We are not alone in responding to the magnetism of our birthplace, for calves, long after they have been put out into a field, will stray into the yard and settle contentedly in the pen where they spent their infancy; and goslings, after weeks of following a hen mother over the orchard grass and sleeping with the other families in the shed, suddenly rediscover the coop where they were brooded, and crowd happily into their first nest, until, some uncalculated desire fulfilled, they desert it as impulsively as they took possession.

It was immediately clear, when we drove into his yard, that Stephen was out, and, most likely, Richeldis also. A particular kind of inertia settles down on a farm during the master's temporary absence: a pall of uneasy boredom descends.

Cows, fidgeting outside the crowded gate, waiting to come in for milking, and all the sounds of calves and pigs and poultry nearing feeding time and discouraged by the absence of confirmatory noises of its preparation, made our search of the outbuildings unnecessary. Hopeful, attentive silences broken by exploratory bellowing and cackling and grunting —hungry calves have a way of bleating as though they were hollow—proclaimed: 'Not at Home'. In a way it was a relief to put off meeting Stephen and acclimatize ourselves gradually to the renewal of family exchanges; for there is no doubt that when Richeldis bought the goslings she intended to cultivate the family wasteland, and George's discoveries are the last links in a chain.

What emerged from our visit was the disclosure that our farm is a facsimile of that other: our calf pens and foodstores, shippon and sties and implement sheds, have been shuffled, during the course of years, into the same relative positions, so that on either farm even I might find my way with the certainty of a dreamer.

Both have the same construction: a mixture of cob and granite, thatch and slate, and old patchwork renovations that have weathered until what was casual has become part of the design. Both were built following the local pattern of farmhouse and outbuildings enclosing a yard, and every alteration that has been made to ours has brought it nearer to being a reflection of the other.

Now it is clear why when our shippon was enlarged it was not extended into the foodstores, which would have been a simple operation, but with far more trouble was built out at the farther end. While one brother has pruned or extended his holding according to a remembered image, the other seems never to have found any alterations necessary, and only the minimum of repairs: a strip of galvanized iron here, a patch of cement there.

Everywhere the easy-going, makeshift, serviceable-enough state of Stephen's place reflected the happy-go-lucky character of the master whose jockeyish figure in breeches and gaiters, cap slanted above a shrewd, convivial face, is more likely to be seen at a race meeting than a market if the fixtures were to coincide; a whippy little man, seasoned by good times as well as bad, while his brother has weathered as a tree will that stands in the teeth of prevalent gales, its growth curtailed on the windward side, its strength concentrated underground.

When seedlings are transplanted, once over the shock they advance towards a maturity which those that are left undisturbed have no incentive to achieve. With their necessity to make root they take on a new lease of life in order to survive. It is not by chance, I believe, that our holding has become an example of careful management which leaves its model far behind, nor, with my sight's partial failure, that the shifted roots of perception have gone down with a fresh impulse to take hold.

All my life I have vaguely hankered after something beyond observation, some means, beyond mere seeing, of penetrating the barrier between beauty and its expression in words.

Once, while Pamela was reading my diaries aloud, Simon came into their family-treasurehouse of a kitchen, possibly in search of something, probably just to reassure himself among his own possessions. He wandered round, touching things, and as he drifted out he asked: 'Did you used to write things down, Luce? I mean when you could see properly?'

I told him that I used to, in an off-and-on way.

'Funny,' he said. 'I'd have thought farming was enough.'

So it was, up to a point. Often, for a long time, just being in the swim was enough, going along with the day's work. Then would come an idea, some sudden illumination of a well-known place or event, but when I tried to capture it with words it would drop like a stone.

This, though impossible to explain, I attempted to lay before Simon, whose triumph was assured from the start.

'Well, then, what d'you try for?'

Because occasionally, very rarely, while the idea hovers it lets fall a feather, a phrase that slides into mind out of the vision itself.

When I began this book as a record of what I saw and remembered I hardly knew what my purpose was. But harvests are reaped for spending in various ways. Transformed into a form of currency, a year's gathering has paid for the assurance that it is not essential to see to the horizon to enjoy what flowers are within reach.

When, as a child, I was taught to say 'For what we are about to receive', and 'For what we have received', 'may the Lord make us truly thankful,' it sufficed. Children have the gift of living in the present. O may I remember to add 'For what we are receiving'.

68

The haylift is out, and my father pursues his leisurely course on the tractor, hauling up the load and paying out the line. Swaths of mown grass cushion my footfall on waves: Braille for seeing the fields like a painted sea. Under the bright sky and light wind the atmosphere is traditional, Archie and Dick gossiping, during pauses, with the Sexton, who has come to help.

'Then I got out me templicate.' The Sexton picks up a theme that a spurt of energy on Dick's part had forced him to lay aside. 'But 'twern't long enough for he.'

Father knows better than to order settled rests; it would take too long to get the old men started again. But from time to time he stops the tractor and combs the rick.

Then Dick lets go of his line and gingerly straightens his back. He knows that the thing is not called a templicate, but he is too polite to correct the Sexton. 'What's the usual size of a grave?'

The Sexton, on the rick, answers with professional briskness: 'Head eighteen inches, shoulders twenty-four, feet sixteen, length six foot seven.'

'Cor.' Dick is prepared for the answer, which he must know from years of lending the Sexton a hand. ''Tain't long enough for I. Have to get a new templament, time I die.'

There can hardly be more than a year or two's difference between the three of them, but no one disputes Dick's claim to the attention due to seniority, and the Sexton assures him that he need not worry; when the time comes he will add a few inches beyond the length of his template.

Archie, attempting to turn the conversation away from the disconcertingly suggestive line it has taken, heads it off.

'You ain't going to die yet, Dicky. 'Twouldn' be the same wi'out ee.'

"Twouldn' be no different, really,' reflects the Sage. 'You'd still be the same yourselves, see.'